FENG SHUI & DESTINY
for FAMILIES

The Indispensable Guide for Every Home

Raymond Lo

TIMES BOOKS INTERNATIONAL
Singapore • Kuala Lumpur

Published by Times Books International
an imprint of Times Editions Pte Ltd
Times Centre
1 New Industrial Road
Singapore 536196
Fax: (65) 2854871 Tel: (65) 2848844
E-mail: te@corp.tpl.com.sg
Online Book Store: http://www.timesone.com.sg/te

Times Subang
Lot 46, Subang Hi-Tech Industrial Park
Batu Tiga
40000 Shah Alam
Selangor Darul Ehsan
Malaysia
Fax & Tel: (603) 7363517
E-mail: cchong@tpg.com.my

Printed in Singapore

ISBN 981 204 040 4

Acknowledgements

I must thank Ms Shirley Hew of Times Editions for proposing the idea for this book to me. She is a lovely mother who is very anxious about the well-being of her children.

Over the past couple of years, the Hong Kong Tourist Association has allowed me considerable exposure to the foreign media, and I thank them for offering me such good opportunities to introduce feng shui to the world.

My thanks also to Ms Jennifer Yin, whose phone call one morning in 1996 set in motion a string of coincidences that led to an opportunity to introduce feng shui to the participants at the World Economic Forum in Davos in 1997. The very warm reception from the audience gave me the drive to write this book.

I am grateful to all my supporters of my previous books. I offer them my sincere apologies if some of the contents have not been easy to understand. I have tried my best to improve in this book, and I welcome readers to e-mail questions to me if necessary. My e-mail address is raymond@raymond-lo.com.

You are also welcome to visit my web site for information about the courses I offer. My website address is:

http://www.raymond-lo.com

The portraits of famous people in this book were skilfully drawn by the Chinese artist Mr Shek Chun.

Lastly, I want to thank my wife Maureen and my son Justin for their full and unceasing support in my unconventional choice of career.

Contents

Feng Shui

Appendices

Preface

In recent years, the subject of Chinese metaphysics has generated considerable interest among people not just in Asia, but also in the West. The Internet has play an important role in promoting this interest worldwide. If one looks up 'feng shui' on the search engine, he will be pleasantly surprised to discover many websites giving various information on the subject. Many non-Chinese feng shui practitioners advertise on the Internet, and many feng shui organisations and societies have been formed in Europe.

The Internet offers tremendous convenience in communication. But at the same time, wrong information can also spread quickly. While good feng shui masters can offer genuine knowledge through the Web, unscrupulous people whose only intention is to cash in on the strong interest can do likewise too. Therefore, we find much false information on the Internet about feng shui and Chinese metaphysics.

Although it is encouraging to receive hundreds of queries from all over the world, it is frustrating to observe that many questions arise from misconceptions about the subject. This is very unfortunate. If the students experiment with the wrong information, they will be disappointed when the result does not match what is promised. They will lose faith in the subject and conclude that feng shui is merely superstition. This is a serious threat to the future of genuine feng shui practice.

The only way to rescue feng shui from the flood of misleading information is to publicise more honest and logical concepts about the subject. This is the main purpose of my continuing effort to write about Chinese metaphysical subjects and to conduct feng shui and destiny analysis courses.

My last book *Feng Shui and Destiny for Managers* received some good comments from keen feng shui students all over the world. This encouraged me to follow up with this book to cover another important aspect of our lives – matters relating to love, relationships, marriage and children. In the course of my day-to-day feng shui practice, I found that most of my clients want to understand the prospect of their love affairs, their marriage lives and the wellbeing of their children. So the topics in this book have been chosen from the most frequently asked questions of my clients.

This book is dedicated to young people who are looking forward to love affairs and marriage, married couples interested to learn more about conjugal relationships, and mothers anxious to know about their children's health and future. The contents cover matters of common interest: it talks about our day-to-day affairs of love, emotions, health and relationships, and can be a good guide to understand yourself and the people around you.

This book has been written for the general reader. No previous knowledge of feng shui is needed to appreciate the contents. The language has been kept as non-technical as possible and any technical terminology will be explained when they first appear. However, as this is a book you can put into practice after thoroughly understanding its contents, some parts are rather complicated and need to be fully digested and memorised before you can move on to the next section. It may appear difficult at the first reading, but you will find it rewarding to go through a chapter one more time and memorise the concepts introduced. I have derived great joy and pleasure in learning this subject, and I hope you too can share the same happiness.

DESTINY

Knowing Yourself Through the Four Pillars of Destiny

The famous teacher of war strategy, Sun Tzu, once said, "Victory in battle begins with knowing yourself and knowing your enemy." So let us begin this journey by examining ourselves.

If we are confronted with the question, 'How much do you know about yourself?', we can usually talk about our educational background, profession, interests, hobbies, and even personality. But are you truly confident that this is the real YOU? Are you sure others view you the same way you look at yourself? If your friend provides an objective description of you, you may disagree and challenge him that he does not fully understand the real you. The image you project to the world may not match who you think you are.

So who is the real you? No matter how well you feel you understand yourself, most of us have doubts. Even if you are very sure of yourself, how about the future? Will you be the same person tomorrow? If you have such doubts about your true self, I want to offer you a possible solution. That is, your objective self is reflected in the elements that constitute your body and soul, and you can find out the components of your self by an ancient Chinese technique called the 'Four Pillars of Destiny'.

What is Destiny?

The Four Pillars of Destiny is the first metaphysical tool that I would like to introduce in this book. It is a system for destiny analysis – for knowing ourselves, for understanding our strengths, weaknesses, personality, directions in life, and the ups and downs of our fortune cycles in the past, present and future.

The Four Pillars of Destiny is a profound system for destiny analysis. The underlying philosophy is that there are five basic driving forces in the Universe. These basic forces are described in terms of five basic elements – metal, wood, water, fire and earth. The system assumes that everything in the Universe, all matters and all events, including human destiny, is composed of these five basic elements. Like the study of chemistry, various compositions of these five elements will bring about different forms of matter, lives and a large variety of human destiny.

Such elements possess two important qualities: they change over time in cyclical manner and they are not chaotic but interact with one another according to some basic laws. So we have a simple and orderly model of a Universe with nothing but five elements continuously interacting with one another to bring about progress, changes, new matters, new events and new lives. As the five elements follow a cyclical pattern and they react with one another in accordance with fixed laws, an understanding of the cyclical pattern and basic laws or orders allows us to understand lives and forecast the future.

This is a very simple outline of the philosophy behind the system of the Four Pillars of Destiny. Let us now examine the system in more detail.

Any forecast of the future is made under the assumption that there is an order or laws governing the development of any object. Take, for example, classical scientists. They believe that we can forecast the future position of an object if we know its initial position and the laws governing its velocity. So it is quite easy to calculate the position of a cannon ball a few seconds after it is fired. Destiny analysis is a forecasting technique built on the same principle – that we assume life and destiny are governed by natural rules or orders. These rules are the principle of yin and yang and the five basic elements.

The Tai Chi symbolising yin and yang

Modern Western cosmology assumes that the Universe began with the Big Bang. Before the Big Bang, the Universe was in a state of infinite density called a singularity. Then there was a sudden explosion which generated tremendous heat and the energies were released. Matters were formed together with the change in temperature and expansion of the Universe. This theory is similar to ancient Chinese belief. In the teachings of Tao, the Universe was in a state of 'Ultimate Nothingness' before the beginning. Then came a sudden change; not an explosion, but a split into two aspects – yin and yang. These are the Chinese words representing the duality of matter. Every matter has two sides – the positive and the negative, the male and the female, the light and the dark. Thereafter, the five basic elements appeared to create matters. These five elements are symbolised by five common objects we see on earth – metal, wood, water, fire and earth. However, the real meaning of these elements is that they are the five basic forces, or energies in nature, that are the basic components or constituents of all matters in the Universe.

The five elements:

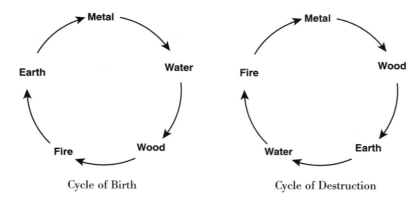

Cycle of Birth   Cycle of Destruction

These five elements are not chaotic. They are related to one another by two basic laws presented in the form of two cycles. The Cycle of Birth shows the harmonious mother-and-child relationship with one element giving birth to another. The Cycle of Destruction shows the more hostile type of relationship, with one element controlling or destroying the other.

These two simple cycles are considered the basic laws of nature that govern the relationships, changes and progress of all matters and events in the Universe.

Just as all matters in the Universe are made up of the five basic elements, so too is man and his destiny. Each of us is also composed of the various combinations of elements and our fortune and destiny are governed by the basic laws of nature – the Cycle of Birth and the Cycle of Destruction. If we find out and understand the composition of elements in ourselves, it becomes possible to understand our nature better and to look into our future.

The Chinese Calendar

How can we know what are the component elements which make up our body and also our destiny? The Chinese have invented an ingenious calendar system which provides a link between man and the Universe.

The Western calendar is only a numeral record of time; it is merely a series of numbers which tells nothing but the progression of time. The Chinese calendar, on the other hand, not only serves this purpose, but also carries information about the five basic elements. From the Chinese calendar, one not only gets a record of time, but also understands what elements are prevailing or dominating during a particular moment.

Take, for example, the year 1996. In the Chinese calendar, this is represented by the two Chinese characters 丙子. The first character, called heavenly stem, is a symbol of the yang fire element. The second character, called the earthly branch, is a symbol of the yang water element. It tells us that the elements of fire and water are the dominating elements in the Universe during 1996.

From the Cycle of Birth and the Cycle of Destruction, one can derive considerable meaning from this fire-and-water combination. The Cycle of Destruction tells us that water will destroy fire. Hence the first impression we get from a fire-water combination is that these are conflicting elements. This implies that the world will not be in harmony in 1996. Indeed, one can easily recall hostilities between the United States and Iraq, Beijing and Taiwan, China and Japan, North and South Korea, and the IRA and the British Government, just to mention a few examples.

The conflict between fire and water also implies natural disasters related to these elements. For example, there was severely cold weather in many places: in the United States and in Hong Kong (where many elderly people died from the cold). China and North Korea were hit by floods. Two planes collided over India (fire), the Gartley Building fire in Hong Kong killed 40 people and the bulk carrier mv Bright Field brought down a shopping mall on the banks of the Mississippi river.

Fire and water together means the fire is weak and the water is strong. Fire is the element related to lighting, power and energy, so there was a massive power failure in the United States and in Malaysia in 1996. Fire is also related to the heart and the blood in the human body, so there were more heart troubles reported in 1996. One prominent example was President Boris Yeltsin of Russia, who had to undergo a heart operation.

These are just simple examples to demonstrate how the five basic elements reflected in the Chinese calendar system can be used as a handy and accurate forecasting tool. So far we have only considered the year, but the Chinese calendar system can also express the month, the day and the hour, each in terms of two elements. As such, we can translate any moment in time into elemental form and see what bundle of basic elements are prevailing at that particular moment.

The birth data of a person provides very important information. If you translate the birth data – the year, month, day and hour – into the Chinese calendar, you obtain four pairs of Chinese characters, each representing two elements. Therefore, you get a bundle of eight Chinese characters showing the eight elements prevailing at birth. These eight Chinese characters – representing the influence of eight elements – symbolise the elemental composition of the person and reflect his destiny.

As mentioned earlier, in the Chinese calendar system, each piece of information about time is represented by two Chinese characters. One is called the heavenly stem and the other the earthly branch. These stems and branches are like numbers; they follow one another in a set sequence. There are altogether 10 heavenly stems and 12 earthly branches. Each represents an element as shown in the following table. These 22 Chinese characters are all you need to operate the Chinese calendar as well as the system of destiny analysis called the Four Pillars of Destiny.

Heavenly Stems		Earthly Branches	
甲	Yang wood	子	Water (Mouse)
乙	Yin wood	丑	Earth (Ox)
丙	Yang fire	寅	Wood (Tiger)
丁	Yin fire	卯	Wood (Rabbit)
戊	Yang earth	辰	Earth (Dragon)
己	Yin earth	巳	Fire (Snake)
庚	Yang metal	午	Fire (Horse)
辛	Yin metal	未	Earth (Ram)
壬	Yang water	申	Metal (Monkey)
癸	Yin water	酉	Metal (Rooster)
		戌	Earth (Dog)
		亥	Water (Pig)

The 10 heavenly stems and 12 earthly branches

From the table, you can observe that the heavenly stems and earthly branches do not just incorporate the system of the five elements. They also include the concept of yin and yang: one stem represents yang wood while another represents yin wood. When pairing the stems with the branches, the rule is that a yang stem must pair up with a yang branch and a yin stem can only team up with a yin branch. The maximum possible number of combinations of heavenly stems and earthly branches is only 60. Any moment in time can be expressed in terms of four pairs of heavenly stems and earthly branches taken from these 60 pairs. These four pairs of stems and branches express the elements prevailing at a particular hour, on a particular day, in a certain month and in a certain year. Hence this system of fortune-telling is commonly known as the Four Pillars of Destiny.

A Born Entertainer

At this juncture, it is best to demonstrate with a practical example of a child born on 18 February 1954. This birth data, when converted into the Chinese calendar, is as follows:

HOUR	DAY	MONTH	YEAR
癸 Water	乙 Wood	丙 Fire	甲 Wood
未 Earth	巳 Fire	寅 Wood	午 Fire

The Pillars of Destiny of a man born on 18/2/54 at 2.50 p.m.

Each of the items of year, month, day and hour, when expressed in the Chinese calendar, become symbols of elements. We can immediately see the composition of elements in our moment of birth which exactly reflects the elemental components of our destiny. In our example, the boy has many fire elements, some wood elements as well as some water elements. How do we read his destiny in such a random bundle of elements? The first step is to look at the day of birth. The element on top of the day pillar, called the heavenly stem, represents the person himself. In this case, the wood element shows that, by definition, this person is a man of wood. The wood element on the day pillar represents his self. The elements in the other pillars represent his environment, the people in his life, and various aspects of human life, such as money, power and status, intelligence and skill, colleagues and enemies, resources and knowledge and so on. By examining the group of elements in the Four Pillars of birth year, month, day and hour, we can study the destiny of a person in detail.

In our sample birth data, the man is a man of wood. His Four Pillars have three wood elements and one water element, which are all supportive of wood. We can conclude that the self element wood is rather strong. If a wood person has many other wood elements in his destiny, it means that he sees many other people, in other words, the public. This is somewhat related to the mass media.

The second strongest element in the Four Pillars appears to be fire. There are three fire elements. As wood gives birth to fire, fire is a symbol of creativity and intelligence expressed by a wood person. The strong presence of fire indicates that this person is presentable and creative.

Let us now look at the other elements. Besides wood and fire, there is one water and one earth element in the hour pillar. According to the Cycle of Birth, water gives birth to wood. Water is thus a symbol of resources and knowledge to a wood person. However the single water element is weak as it is exhausted by wood. This shows that the person will not impress with his academic achievements.

Let us look at the earth element. Earth is the element conquered by wood, according to the Cycle of Destruction. If a person conquers an object, the object is his reward. Therefore, the earth element, to a wood person, symbolises his reward, or his material wealth. This symbol of money, which appears in the earthly branch of the Four Pillars, indicates that the person possesses money. But as this money is not particularly prominent, the person is not overly commercial. People will not regard him as a man of money.

We have already examined four of the five basic elements. There is only one element left: the metal element. Metal is totally absent from this set of destiny. Metal is the destroyer of wood and so symbolises restriction, discipline, power and status to a wood person. Why is this so? Let us assume the element that destroys or controls a person's self element creates a burden on a person. If this person is an employee in an organisation, the burden can mean a heavy workload and many responsibilities. If heavy responsibilities are assigned to an employee, there usually comes with such duties a title or status so that this person can do his work with authority.

For example, if you are asked to manage a group of workers, the company should give you the title of supervisor or manager. Your heavy burden turns out to be your power and status. Therefore, the element that destroys the self actually symbolises power and status. Another way to understand this concept is to simply consider the element controlling the self as symbolising laws and restrictions, and laws and restrictions as representing power and discipline. Hence the element controlling the self is regarded as a symbol of power.

Returning to our example of the man born on 18 February 1954, the metal element, representing power and status, is totally absent. This shows that this person's career has nothing to do with power or status. He will not be a politician or a manager.

From the combination of elements reflected in this set of birth data, we are given strong signals as to what type of person this man is. He is smart and presentable, with good public performance skills. He is not a commercial man; he does not impress others with his academic achievements and knowledge; he is not a managerial type. Yet he can reach out to the public and make a living with his skill ...

Who is he? He is the popular Hollywood movie star Mr John Travolta, who rocketed to fame with his impressive dancing in the hit movie *Saturday Night Fever*. His great performing skills and celebrity are all written in the elemental composition of his destiny.

17

MARRIAGE

Starting a Romance

In the last chapter, I briefly introduced the technique of the Four Pillars of Destiny. Through understanding the composition of the elements within our destiny, as expressed by our birth data, the technique offers deep insight into the forces which bring about our personality, career directions, up and down cycles in life, health, marriage, relationships with people and many other matters.

To carry out a destiny analysis, a few essential steps must be followed. First, your birth data must be converted from the Western calendar to the Chinese Hsia calendar. To do this, a tool called *The Thousand Year Calendar* is used. This contains both the Hsia calendar and the equivalent Western calendar between the years 1912 to 2029. An English version of *The Thousand Year Calendar* can be found in the book *Discover Your Destiny* by Ms Hee Yin Fan, published by Times Books International. However, it is not difficult to use the Chinese version, if you can get hold of it. Appendix 1 will guide you on how to use the Chinese version of the calendar.

The Luck Pillars

After you have listed out your Four Pillars of Destiny in terms of the heavenly stems and earthly branches, the next step is to list out another series of elements called the luck pillars. The luck pillars are pairs of elements which affect a person's life and fortune in ten-year periods. Once a person is born, he begins his journey through life. At each stage of his passage, he encounters different kinds of elemental influences which either cause good fortune or obstacles. These elemental influences are reflected in the luck pillars. Each luck pillar contains two elements that affect the person for ten years, causing ups and downs in life. On top of each luck pillar there is also a number which shows the age when the person comes under the influence of the luck pillar. The age at which the journey through each luck pillar begins varies, depending on how close the person's date of birth is to the beginning or the end of the month of birth.

The luck pillars reflect a cycle in life. As cyclical changes are best represented by the seasonal changes experienced by people, the luck pillars are, therefore, derived from the month of birth which reflects the season when the person is born. A guide to list out the luck pillars and the formula to find the age to start each luck pillar can be found in Appendix 2.

After you have converted your Western birth data into the Hsia calendar format and listed out the series of luck pillars, interpretation and analysis can begin. The first step to understanding a set of Four Pillars of Destiny is to examine the element representing the self. This is the heavenly stem of the day pillar, where the self element is located. For example, if you are born on a day with wood heavenly stem, you are a wood person.

The other seven Chinese characters, each representing an element, are regarded as people surrounding the self. Each Chinese character occupies a position in the Four Pillars, symbolising a category of relationship in our life. As a general rule, the year pillar represents the more distant relations, for example, the grandparents. The month pillar is closer to the self and so refers to the parents. The heavenly stem of the month pillar, in particular, symbolises the father. As for the day pillar, the heavenly stem represents the self while the earthly branch represents the spouse, either the husband or the wife. The hour pillar symbolises the children.

With this understanding of the positional meanings of the Four Pillars, it is easy to examine relationships between the self and other people in our lives. Take an example where the self element is wood and the heavenly stem of the month pillar is metal. According to the Cycle of Destruction, metal destroys wood. This indicates that the person has a harsh father who exercises discipline and control over the child. You can also examine the relationship between husband and wife. If the self element is wood and the earthly branch of the day pillar is water, this usually symbolises a harmonious relationship, with the spouse giving the self love and support. But if the earthly branch is metal, the spouse can be domineering, with a wish to control the self.

The Humble Beginnings of Li Ka-shing

To demonstrate, let us examine the following Four Pillars of Destiny.

HOUR	DAY	MONTH	YEAR
?	甲 Wood	戊 Earth	戊 Earth
?	申 Metal	午 Fire	辰 Earth

The Pillars of Destiny of Hong Kong tycoon Mr Li Ka-shing

The heavenly stem of the day pillar is wood. Hence this is a wood person. The wood is surrounded by very strong earth and fire elements. According to the Cycle of Birth and Cycle of Destruction, wood conquers earth and generates fire. Both actions of conquering and generating other elements require energy. Thus both the earth and fire elements exhaust the energy of the wood element. As the earth and fire in the month pillar symbolise the position of the parents, and are unhelpful to the wood, we can conclude that this person is from a poor family, whose parents could not offer him comfort during childhood or help his career.

This is the destiny of renowned Hong Kong tycoon Mr Li Ka-shing. Mr Li was born to a poor family, and after his father passed away while he was still a boy, he had to move to Hong Kong to earn a living as a factory worker.

This method of examining the position of each element to determine relationships is only an elementary step for beginners. A more in-depth method to study relationships is to represent each category of relatives by elements, in accordance with the Cycle of Destruction and Cycle of Birth. Take, for example, a wood person. Water gives birth to wood so water is the element symbolising the mother to a wood person.

In this way, the elements can be used to represent all types of relationships. If a man is born on a day in which the heavenly stem is wood, he is a wood man. Water gives birth to wood, so his mother is water. Traditionally, man is the stronger sex that conquers the woman. As wood conquers earth, earth is the symbol of his wife. Earth gives birth to metal according to the Cycle of Birth. Metal thus symbolises the wood man's children. Earth symbolises his father as earth conquers water, the symbol of his mother, in the same way a husband conquers his wife. The man's sisters and brothers are of the same category and status and so are symbolised by wood.

Deriving Other Relationships Through Logic

You can also derive indirect relationships by exercising your logic. For example you may want to know what element represents the father-in-law. The father-in-law is the father of the wife. As the wife is symbolised by the earth element, her mother is the element which gives birth to earth – fire. The father-in-law is the husband to the mother of the wife, symbolised by the element that conquers fire, so he is represented by the water element.

In this example, we have seen how to derive various relatives for a man of the wood element. Using the same method, you should be able to deduce the same for persons of all other elements. It is useful to carry out this exercise to familiarise yourself with the elemental relationships. However, for the sake of convenience, a table showing the relatives for persons of every element is provided in Appendix 3.

At this stage, you may have noticed that I have introduced two ways of examining relationships with other people. The first method is to look at the position of the Four Pillars. The second method is to classify different types of people by the elements.

The first method is called the 'House method'. For example, the heavenly stem of the month pillar is the 'House of the Father' and the earthly branch of the day pillar is the 'House of the Spouse'. This method is best for examining relationships with the self. The second method, the 'element method', on the other hand, categorises different people in our lives by elemental relationships.

Why we do need two systems of looking at relatives? The reason is that each system shows different aspects of relationships. The 'House method' is handy to see the relationship with the self but is not good enough to examine that particular category of relative in more detail. For example, every set of Four Pillars has a 'House of Spouse' as it is merely the earthly branch of the day pillar. However, it does not mean everyone will get married just because they have a 'House of Spouse'. There are many who do not have a spouse. So this aspect of whether you will marry or not cannot be revealed by the 'House of Spouse'. You have to examine whether the person possesses the element representing the spouse in his Four Pillars of Destiny. In the case of a wood man, if he has strong earth elements, his chances of getting married are greater than one without any earth element.

This is just a simple example of how we can use both methods to examine a relationship. We will look at some case studies later in this book.

Finding the
Right Partner

The 'House' and 'element' methods reveal your relationship with a particular category of person by examining your own Four Pillars of Destiny. However, it takes two to tango. When you talk about compatibility in human relationships, it is necessary to examine a pair of Four Pillars of Destiny.

From our own experiences, some people seem to have a certain charm and are more attractive to us than others. Amongst your friends there are always some whom you feel are easier to get along with and are quicker to develop friendships. These are people with whom we find a stronger degree of compatibility.

In the philosophy of the Four Pillars of Destiny, one major factor of compatibility is the complementary relationship. This means you are attracted to another person because he or she possesses something you need. If he is also attracted to you, in most cases, this also means you possess something he wants.

Each of us is made up of different elemental components as reflected in our Four Pillars of Destiny. Some of us have many earth elements but lack water; others may have too much metal and lack fire, and so on. Very often, there is an imbalance and inadequacy in our composition of elements in our Four Pillars. We need additional elements to help bring balance and harmony to our original composition of elements. These additional elements are called 'favourable elements'.

Li Ka-shing

Let us look at Mr Li Ka-shing's Four Pillars again. Mr Li is a wood person surrounded by earth and fire, which exhaust the wood's energy. There is an imbalance in his destiny. His wood element is weak and he needs support to keep the excessive earth and fire under control. Such support comes from the water element. According to the Cycle of Birth, water gives birth to wood. Hence water will strengthen the wood and suppress the earth element. Water is therefore the favourable element to Mr Li Ka-shing. Once he encounters the wood element, which occurs after the age of 38, he will be in balance and good fortune will come to him.

HOUR	DAY	MONTH	YEAR
?	甲 Wood	戊 Earth	戊 Earth
?	申 Metal	午 Fire	辰 Earth

68	58	48	38	28	18	8
乙 Wood	甲 Wood	癸 Water	壬 Water	辛 Metal	庚 Metal	己 Earth
丑 Earth	子 Water	亥 Water	戌 Earth	酉 Metal	申 Metal	未 Earth

The Pillars of Destiny of Mr Li Ka-shing

In the case of Mr Li, water is his favourable element. However, water also needs support from metal. As such, metal is called the 'second best' element. Wood, which helps control the excessive amount of earth, is also a good element.

On the other hand, as earth is already excessive, any encounter with more earth elements will upset the balance. Earth is the 'unfavourable element'. Fire supports earth, so fire is the 'second worst element' as it will make the earth element even more excessive.

From this example, we can see that favourable elements are those that bring balance to the elements in a set of Four Pillars. Unfavourable elements are those that cause more imbalance, making an excessive element more excessive or a weak element weaker. The general guideline is that when the self element is weak, favourable elements are those that give birth to or support the self element. Unfavourable elements are those that exhaust or suppress the self element. If the self element is too strong, then the favourable elements are those that help exhaust the excessive energy of the self element, while the unfavourable elements are those that generate more of the self element, increasing its strength.

25

For example, if the self element is fire, and it is born in a season of water (making it quite weak), then the favourable element will be wood which supports the fire and makes it stronger. Metal exhausts the fire and is unfavourable. If some wood is present in the Four Pillars, then the second best element is water as it supports the favourable element wood which supports the fire. The second unfavourable element is earth which exhausts the fire and supports the bad element – metal. However, if the fire self element is strong, born in a season of wood or fire, then the favourable elements will be earth and metal which help reduce the fire energy, while the unfavourable elements will be wood and water which strengthen the already excessive fire energy.

The basic rule is to find some supportive elements when the self is weak and some exhaustive elements when the self is strong. However, there is one major exception to this rule. This manner of finding the favourable and unfavourable elements only applies to ordinary sets of Four Pillars, that is when the self element is weak, but not extremely weak, or strong but not strong to the extreme.

'Follow the Leader': President Bill Clinton

Another set of guidelines is applicable when the self element is weak or strong to the extreme. Let us look at the following example:

HOUR	DAY	MONTH	YEAR
庚 Metal	乙 Wood	丙 Fire	丙 Fire
辰 Earth	丑 Earth	申 Metal	戌 Earth

67	57	47	37	27	17	7
癸 Water	壬 Water	辛 Metal	庚 Metal	己 Earth	戊 Earth	丁 Fire
卯 Wood	寅 Wood	丑 Earth	子 Water	亥 Water	戌 Earth	酉 Metal

The Pillars of Destiny of President Bill Clinton

These are the Four Pillars of President Bill Clinton of the United States. He was born on a day of wood. By definition he is a wood man. However, his wood element is extremely weak as there is totally no support of water or other wood in his Four Pillars. He falls under the 'extremely weak' category and must be treated differently. We call this type of Four Pillars 'Follow the Leader'.

The idea behind the 'Follow the Leader' concept is that if the self element is extremely weak and has no foundation at all, it cannot survive by itself. It has to submit to the power of the 'leader' in the set of Four Pillars. In President Clinton's case, the leader is the metal element which dominates the month of birth and is supported by three earth elements and one other metal element. A new set of rules for finding the favourable and unfavourable elements now applies. The favourable element is the one which supports the leader, while the unfavourable element is the one which supports the self. The reasoning is that when the self element follows the leader, he will benefit when the leader is strong. If he encounters elements which support the self, the self may want to become independent from the leader. This goes against the principle of 'Follow the Leader' and the self may be punished by misfortunes.

In the case of President Clinton, his favourable elements are earth and metal which support the leader metal while his unfavourable elements are water and wood which support the wood self. President Clinton's greatest success took place after he turned 36, in the luck pillar of metal and earth. In 1992, a year of strong metal, he defeated George Bush to become president of the United States. This shows that metal is his favourable element.

The birth data of many famous people fall under the 'Follow the Leader' category. Notable examples include Mr Deng Xiaoping and Mr John Lennon, both of whom have been covered in my other books.

Establishing the favourable and unfavourable elements for a set of Four Pillars of Destiny is vital to understanding the fortunes of a person. When favourable elements appear in a luck pillar, it usually signifies a period of good fortune. If unfavourable elements appear in the luck pillar or in a particular year, the person should be careful as such unfavourable elements will upset the balance of elements in his destiny.

Knowing a person's favourable and unfavourable elements also serves another very important function – to evaluate compatible relationships. If your favourable element is metal, once you encounter a person whose Four Pillars are strong in metal, you will find the person attractive. Looking for your favourable elements in the other person's destiny is an effective way to assess compatibility in a relationship.

Bruce Willis and Demi Moore

Let us examine the following example:

HOUR	DAY	MONTH	YEAR
?	己 Earth	己 Earth	乙 Wood
?	卯 Wood	卯 Wood	未 Earth

64	54	44	34	24	14	4
壬 Water	癸 Water	甲 Wood	乙 Wood	丙 Fire	丁 Fire	戊 Earth
申 Metal	酉 Metal	戊 Earth	亥 Water	子 Water	丑 Earth	寅 Wood

The Pillars of Destiny of Mr Bruce Willis (19/3/55)

HOUR	DAY	MONTH	YEAR
?	癸 Water	辛 Metal	壬 Water
?	丑 Earth	亥 Water	寅 Wood

61	51	41	31	21	11	1
甲 Wood	乙 Wood	丙 Fire	丁 Fire	戊 Earth	己 Earth	庚 Metal
辰 Earth	巳 Fire	午 Fire	未 Earth	申 Metal	酉 Metal	戌 Earth

The Pillars of Destiny of Ms Demi Moore (11/11/62)

These pillars of destiny belong to a famous couple in Hollywood – Mr Bruce Willis and Ms Demi Moore. Let us examine their compatibility. Ms Demi Moore was born on a day of water in a month of water. She is thus a strong water lady. Her water is supported by metal which makes it even stronger. Her favourable elements are those that provide an outlet for her excessive water energy and help her reduce the strength of water. Such elements are wood, fire and earth which can exhaust or suppress the energy of water. Metal and water, which strengthen her water energy, are her unfavourable elements.

Ms Moore has been under the influence of the favourable elements of fire and earth since she turned 31. During this period she acted in several very successful movies

Bruce Willis, born on a day of earth, is an earth man. This earth is surrounded by very strong wood and water. As wood conquers earth and water gives birth to wood, both the wood and water elements will exhaust the strength of the earth element. Hence his earth is weak. Under normal circumstances, weak earth requires the support of fire. However, in Mr Willis' three known pillars of destiny, the fire element is totally absent. His earth element is weak to the extreme, so he is a 'Follow the Leader' type. His 'leader' is wood, the strongest element in his destiny.

As explained earlier, the rule for this type of destiny is that any element that supports the leader is favourable while any element that supports the self is unfavourable. Mr Willis' favourable element is water which supports his leader – wood. His unfavourable element is fire which supports his earth self.

As Ms Moore possesses very strong water in her destiny, this meets the need of Mr Willis. On the other hand, Ms Moore needs wood as an outlet for her excessive water energy. Again she is able to find very strong wood in Mr Willis' destiny. This complementary relationship creates a strong attraction between Ms Moore and Mr Willis. This is exactly how we consider compatibility in human relationships.

This phenomenon of complementary elemental relationships between two partners is not only commonly observed between married couples. Such relationships are also found between parents and children. Very often, the Four Pillars of Destiny of the first child to a couple carry much of the elements favourable to the mother or father. For example, if the father lacks metal, then his first child's destiny often has a large amount of metal that meets the father's needs.

Marriage: When is a Good Time?

In the last chapter we have examined how we can determine compatibility between two persons. The basic criterion for a good relationship is that each person in the partnership should possess the favourable elements of the other party. We have observed that Ms Demi Moore's destiny contains plenty of water elements – the favourable element of her husband Mr Bruce Willis. Mr Willis' destiny is, in turn, very strong in the wood element – the favourable element for Ms Moore.

The complementary elements that exist in two persons' destinies are primarily responsible for generating attraction between them. Perhaps the elements are the driving force behind the 'love at first sight' type of romance. However, marriage is much more complicated than mere attraction. We may be attracted to many people during our lives but we usually only have one marriage partner. In traditional Chinese philosophy there is a term called 'yuen', which means the attraction between two persons. There is also another term called 'fan', meaning the chance of getting married. Both 'yuen' and 'fan' must be present before two lovers can get married.

What we have described in the last chapter is the 'yuen'. In this chapter let us examine the 'fan'.

In every set of Four Pillars of Destiny, there are clues which will cast light on the marriage aspect. One major clue is the element that represents the spouse. This element is defined as follows:

- If the self is a man, his wife is the element that he conquers. Example: if the self element is metal, then the element representing the wife is wood which is conquered by metal.
- If the self is a woman, her husband is the element that conquers her. Example: a metal lady's husband is symbolised by fire – the element that conquers metal.

This husband-and-wife relationship is not difficult to remember as it follows the traditional Chinese philosophy that man is the stronger sex that conquers woman, the weaker sex.

Understanding such elemental symbols enables us to recognise the 'fan' when it comes into our lives. If a woman is pondering over her chances of getting married, she only needs to find out which is the element that destroys her self in her destiny and observe when this 'destructive' element, symbolising her husband, appears with significant strength in her luck pillars.

Movie Queen Lin Ching Hsia

Let me demonstrate this technique with an example of a famous marriage.

HOUR	DAY	MONTH	YEAR
辛 Metal	癸 Water	甲 Wood	甲 Wood
酉 Metal	亥 Water	戌 Earth	午 Fire

68	58	48	38	28	18	8
丁 Fire	戊 Earth	己 Earth	庚 Metal	辛 Metal	壬 Water	癸 Water
卯 Wood	辰 Earth	巳 Fire	午 Fire	未 Earth	申 Metal	酉 Metal

The Pillars of Destiny of Ms Lin Ching Hsia

The above set of Four Pillars belongs to movie queen Ms Lin Ching Hsia. She was happily married to a fashion tycoon in Hong Kong in 1994 and gave birth to a baby girl in 1995.

Ms Lin is a lady of water. In the heavenly stems of her year and month pillars are two wood elements. As water gives birth to wood, wood symbolises creativity and intelligence to a water person. Now the heavenly stems often reflect the image and outlook of a person whereas the earthly branches reveal the more subtle inner personality. Thus a person whose intelligence element appears on the heavenly stems of the year and month pillars will come across as smart and presentable – a fundamental requirement for someone in show business. Ms Lin's strong intelligence and creativity element is primarily responsible for her beauty, her superb acting skills and her great successes as an international movie star.

Ms Lin's year and month pillars are occupied by strong earth and wood elements which suppress or exhaust her water. She is thus a weak water lady who needs support from her resource element, metal. Metal and water are her favourable elements. Fortunately Ms Lin has an excellent configuration of these favourable elements in her day and hour pillars. As an actress, Ms Lin must be able to express herself well. Her strong resource element, which symbolises knowledge, education and control and restraint in one's behaviour, enables her to do this well.

From Ms Lin's luck pillars, we can also observe that the favourable metal element first appeared at the age of about 8 and remains strong until the age of 48. This accounts for her great acting successes from an early age.

There are many other aspects that we can examine in a set of Four Pillars of Destiny. But in this chapter, let us just emphasise the marriage aspect.

Ms Lin is a water lady, so the element that symbolises her husband is earth. In Ms Lin's Four Pillars, the earth element is present in the month pillar. This earth is supported by the fire element of the year pillar so it is not weak. We can conclude that she has at least a husband present at her destiny.

After identifying the husband's element in a lady's destiny, the next question is how good is this husband? To examine a husband-and-wife relationship, we need to look at two key areas. First, we should examine the House of Spouse which is the earthly branch of the day pillar.

The relationship between the House of Spouse and the self element usually reflects the relationship between husband and wife. There are many possible configurations of relationships. In the previous example of Mr Li Ka-shing, Mr Li's day pillar is wood over metal. His self element is wood, and the House of Spouse is occupied by metal. As metal destroys wood, this indicates that his wife could be somewhat domineering. However, we should also examine the surrounding elements. In Mr Li's case, the metal is next to the fire element which keeps the metal under control. Therefore, the relationship could be that the wife desires to control the husband but her power is too weak to accomplish this. Nevertheless, as metal is a favourable element to Mr Li, we can conclude that his wife is supportive of him.

Let us now look at Ms Lin's husband-and-wife relationship. Her day pillar is water over water. This means husband and wife are equal in status, with neither side trying to dominate the other. The good point about having the same element in the House of Spouse is that husband and wife will cooperate and live in harmony as both have the same favourable and unfavourable elements. They will encounter good fortune and bad fortune at the same time. Husband and wife will be able to share a phase of good luck and walk hand in hand through a phase of bad luck. Sharing both joy and sorrow in life is an important factor in ensuring a long lasting marriage. If the element of the House of Spouse differs from the element of the self, the favourable element enjoyed by the self may be the unfavourable element for the spouse. This could mean when the husband is in good fortune, the wife is unhappy. Such discrepancy in fortune is often the source of disharmony in a marriage. The water over water configuration of Ms Lin's day pillar shows that she will enjoy a good husband-and-wife relationship.

Also playing an important role in a lady's marriage relationship is the resource element which supports the self. Because a lady's husband is symbolised by the destructive element which destroys the self, this creates a burden on the self element. However, a destructive element becomes 'productive' if the resource element is present. In the case of water lady Ms Lin Ching Hsia, the element representing her husband is earth, the destroyer of water. Earth will exert pressure on the weak water. But if metal, the resource element of water, is present, then earth will give birth to metal which in turn supports water. In this manner, earth will not destroy water, but indirectly give birth to water.

The implication of this in marriage is that in the absence of the resource element in a lady's destiny, she will feel the pressure and burden generated by her husband which is her destructive element. Her husband may be too demanding or too hot tempered, making her feel abused. But if her resource element is present, the destructive element of her husband is transformed into the resource element which provides her with comfort. Thus the presence of the resource element in a lady's destiny is vital to ensure a harmonious marriage relationship. Ms Lin has strong metal in her hour pillar. Because of this, her husband will be kind and gentle to her.

When Will a Lady Get Married?

Let us now go on to the next question – when will a lady get married? If the element representing the husband is present but weak, it is possible that marriage will not happen. A weak husband's element may only lead to romances which do not result in marriage. While the chances for encountering male partners may exist and romances can develop, such partners could be too weak to qualify for a marriage relationship. Weak in the sense that the lady does not find him suitable because of his background, education, status, and so on. To encounter a suitable candidate, the husband's element must be strong. Hence to determine the appropriate time for marriage to take place, we simply need to find the luck pillar during which the husband's element is very strong.

Let us now re-examine Ms Lin's luck pillars to trace her past history of romance and see if we can determine when her chance for marriage will occur.

Ms Lin's husband's element is earth. It is present in the month pillar and supported by fire from the year pillar. So the earth element is not weak. However, Ms Lin encountered plenty of metal and water elements in her first few luck pillars, which exhausted the strength of the earth element. It is obvious that she will not encounter a suitable partner before the age of 28.

After the age of 28, she entered a luck pillar of metal over earth. The earth element has appeared but with metal exhausting its power, it is not very strong. During this period, between the age of 28 and 38, Ms Lin had romances but her partners were not suitable marriage candidates. So she did not get married.

After the age of 38, she entered a new luck pillar with strong fire in the earthly branches. This strong fire element fuelled the earth element and increased its strength. Ms Lin eventually found a strong, qualified husband and announced her marriage to a Hong Kong fashion tycoon in 1994, a year of earth, when she had just turned 40. You may wonder why she waited for another two years after entering the luck pillar of fire at 38. The reason is that both 1992 and 1993 were strong metal and water years which reduced the strength of her earth element. The year 1994 was the first strong earth year after she stepped into the luck pillar of fire. As you can see, the timing as determined by the five basic elements in our destiny cannot be wrong.

Looking into the future of Ms Lin's marriage, the signs are optimistic, with her earth element gathering strength in her next few luck pillars between the age of 48 and 68. This symbolises her husband's continuing success. On the other hand, as earth strengthens, water weakens and the wood element, symbolising her movie career, becomes less significant. This means Ms Lin will gradually retire from the limelight and become a strong supporter of her husband's career.

In this example, we have examined the many factors that bring about a happy marriage as well as the technique to determine the appropriate time for a good marriage. In the next chapter, we can polish our skill by examining some less successful marriages.

Single for Life?

In the last chapter, we examined how the Four Pillars of Destiny reflect compatibility and attraction between two persons. Using the example of Ms Lin Ching Hsia, we determined the factors that influence the timing for a happy marriage. But Ms Lin is a fortunate example; there are many others who seem ill-fated. Many have not been able to find a good marriage partner and so remained single. In this chapter we will examine some less happy examples to see what obstacles block our chance for a good marriage.

The Tragic Death of Teresa Teng

HOUR	DAY	MONTH	YEAR
丁 Fire	庚 Metal	甲 Wood	癸 Water
丑 Earth	戊 Earth	子 Water	巳 Fire

55	45	35	25	15	5
庚 Metal	己 Earth	戊 Earth	丁 Fire	丙 Fire	乙 Wood
午 Fire	巳 Fire	辰 Earth	卯 Wood	寅 Wood	丑 Earth

The Pillars of Destiny of Ms Teresa Teng

In 1996, the Chinese world was shocked by the sudden death of another famous star – the great songbird Ms Teresa Teng. She died of asthma-related heart trouble while on vacation in Thailand. Ms Teng was a hugely talented singer who enjoyed tremendous popularity in Taiwan, China, Hong Kong and many other countries. But though very successful in her career, emotionally she was not happy. Despite many romantic relationships, she remained single all her life.

Ms Teresa Teng was born on 25 December 1953. Her Four Pillars of Destiny reveal that she is a metal lady born in the winter season when water is very strong. As metal gives birth to water, water symbolises her creativity and intelligence. A significant presence of the creative or intelligence element is often found in the destiny of those in show business as singing and acting requires the showing of one's talents. In Ms Teng's Four Pillars, the water element is not only 'in season' but also appears in the heavenly stem of the year pillar. Hence she is able to display her talent well. This is a typical destiny configuration of a popular star.

However, Teresa Teng's metal self is on the weak side. Despite the presence of two earth elements, the support is inadequate as the fire element, symbolising resource to the earth element, is not strong in winter. Ms Teng still needs the fire element to support her earth which in turn supports her metal self.

The fire element is thus an essential pillar of support in her destiny. There are two fire elements in her configuration – one in her year pillar and another in her hour pillar. If fire is the most favourable element helping her to achieve balance, we can deduce that wood is her second best element as it supports fire. To a metal person, fire symbolises status and wood represents money.

In traditional Chinese medicine, each of our vital internal organs is assigned an element. Fire symbolises the heart and blood circulation system, metal represents the lung and breathing system, water is the kidney, wood is the liver, and earth is the stomach and digestive system. The configuration of these elements in our destiny can reflect weaknesses in health. For example, if the metal element is weak in a set of Four Pillars of Destiny, as in Ms Teng's case, it is a sign that the person is susceptible to sicknesses relating to the lung and breathing system. Indeed Ms Teresa Teng is known to have suffered from asthma, a sickness related to the breathing system, since childhood.

If we examine Ms Teng's luck pillars, we can see that she had been in good fortune since young. By the age of 15, she had entered a luck pillar of fire and wood which brought her tremendous success as a pop singer. This phase of good fortune with fire and wood influences continued in her next luck pillar between the age of 25 and 35 as she became the most popular singing star in Taiwan, Hong Kong, China and other Chinese communities.

After the age of 35, she largely retired from the pop scene and seldom appeared in concerts. This drastic change can also be explained in her destiny. At the age of 35, she entered a new luck pillar of strong earth. Earth suppresses water, symbolising an end to her performing career which requires water as an outlet for her talents. Furthermore, earth symbolises the resource element to a metal person. An abundance of the resource element makes a person more relaxed and less aggressive, opting for more comfort.

Unfortunately, the luck pillar of earth also brought an undesirable effect. Earth exhausts fire, a favourable element to Ms Teng. Fire symbolises the heart and blood circulation and is thus linked to the energy level of our body. The weakening of the fire element results in weakness of the heart, poor blood circulation and a low energy level.

This health problem turned serious after 1994. On 8 May 1995 when Ms Teng was on holiday in Thailand, she suddenly fell sick in her hotel. She was rushed to the hospital but was proclaimed dead. She died of a heart attack caused by asthma.

Clues in Her Destiny

How is her death revealed in her Four Pillars? Her death was caused by the weakness in her fire element symbolising her heart and blood circulation. At the age of 41, Ms Teng was in a luck pillar of strong earth which exhausted the strength of her fire. In her Four Pillars, there are only two fire elements – one in the earthly branch of the year pillar, the other in the hour pillar.

Now among the 12 earthly branches, a clash relationship occurs when two earthly branches of conflicting elements encounter each other. The following table shows the clash relationships between pairs of earthly branches:

The clashes between pairs of earthly branches

When two conflicting elements clash, with one destroying the other, some drastic impact can be expected. The most notable clash happens when the earthly branch of the year pillar – commonly known as the animal sign of the birth year – clashes with the earthly branch of a particular year. This situation, traditionally known as 'in clash with the Grand Duke of the Year', can imply great changes or trouble. Ms Teresa Teng was born in the Year of the Snake, and in accordance with the above table, the snake is in clash with the pig. So it came to be that in 1994, the Year of the Pig, Ms Teng was 'in clash with the Grand Duke of the Year'.

This clash is of grave significance as it shows conflict between water and fire. As fire is Ms Teng's favourable element, the elimination of the fire element in Ms Teng's year pillar signifies that she was entering a dangerous year in 1994. When such a clash occurs, the least you can expect is more travelling during that year. But in Ms Teng's case, the impact was much more significant. Let us also examine the date when her tragic death occurred:

HOUR	DAY	MONTH	YEAR
壬 Water	己 Earth	辛 Metal	乙 Wood
申 Metal	亥 Water	巳 Fire	亥 Water

8 May 1995, at about 4 p.m.

The tragedy occurred on 8 May 1995. In the above set of Four Pillars there are two water elements in the earthly branches, symbolised by the Chinese character 亥. This water element, when expressed in terms of animal signs, refers to the pig. With the double presence of the water pig element, the fire snake in Ms Teng's year pillar was under severe clash and the fire was put out. In the hour pillar, there was another strong water element on the heavenly stem. This water killed the remaining fire element in the hour pillar of Ms Teng's destiny. With both fire elements gone, Ms Teng's Four Pillars became greatly unbalanced – this ultimately caused her death. She died of a heart attack resulting from the total demise of her fire elements, her essential pillar of support in her destiny.

When Ms Teng passed away in 1995, she was still single. She had had many romances but none had developed into marriage. This unsuccessful marriage aspect is also reflected in her destiny.

Being a metal lady, the fire element conquering metal is the symbol of her husband. As this element is rather weak in her Four Pillars, we can expect romance or marriage to only occur when the fire element becomes strong. From Ms Teng's luck pillars, we can observe that she encountered the strongest wood and fire influences between the age of 15 and 25. During this period, she met many male admirers and developed numerous romances. However, she was perhaps too young then and was focusing on her singing career, so the chance was not taken. After the age of 25, she entered another phase of fire and wood. However, this is yin fire which is weaker than the yang fire of the previous ten years. Her romances continued but, as the fire power was not as strong as before, the male partners she encountered during this period were not as qualified as those she met before she turned 25. On entering a luck pillar of strong earth after the age of 35, the fire element was further weakened. Her marriage chances simply expired after the age of 35. However, she still had a loyal boyfriend who was considerably younger. This is also a consequence of the weak fire element, symbolising a weaker (in terms of age) male partner.

In this example we have seen that our luck pillars can reveal the best time to marry. In Ms Teng's case, this was the period before age 35. An understanding of our Four Pillars thus serves as a useful guide for making an important decision like marriage. If Ms Teng had realised that her marriage prospect after age 35 would be so poor, she might well have chosen to marry before then.

Why Marriages Break Down

We have so far examined how our Four Pillars of Destiny can reveal much information about our marriage prospects. From the examples of Ms Lin Ching Hsia and Ms Teresa Teng, we also observed that the timing of marriage depends on several complicated factors in our destiny.

In the case of Ms Lin, we can predict that her marriage will be stable and lasting as the element representing her husband – the power and status element – will remain strong for a long time. However, Ms Lin is a very fortunate example who has succeeded in both her career and marriage. There are many others who are not so lucky. A careful study of some of the tragic examples will offer us a deeper insight into marriage relationships and allow us to find out the problems that can turn a good marriage sour. In this chapter let us examine perhaps the most sensational court case in American history – the O. J. Simpson trial.

Ms Nicole Brown, the separated wife of Hollywood celebrity and football star Mr O. J. Simpson, was found murdered on 12 June 1994. Her husband was subsequently charged with murder and the trial, which eventually resulted in the acquittal of Mr Simpson of murder charges in 1995, created great controversy in the United States. The Four Pillars of Destiny can also be applied as a tool to help resolve mysteries and can offer clues as to what really happened. However, this is not the theme of this book. So in this chapter let us focus on the marriage relationship and see what caused such a tragic end to a seemingly happy marriage relationship.

Nicole Brown and O. J. Simpson

First let us look at the Four Pillars of Destiny of Ms Nicole Brown. She was born on 19 May 1959, which can be translated into the following heavenly stems and earthly branches:

HOUR	DAY	MONTH	YEAR
?	辛 Metal	己 Earth	己 Earth
?	丑 Earth	巳 Fire	亥 Water

36	26	16	6
癸 Water	壬 Water	辛 Metal	庚 Metal
酉 Metal	申 Metal	未 Earth	午 Fire

The Pillars of Destiny of Ms Nicole Brown

Ms Brown is a metal lady with plenty of earth elements. Despite being born in the summer when the strong fire threatens the metal, we can still regard her metal as strong. This is because the fire element would have been exhausted by the plentiful earth in its surroundings. As Ms Brown's self is too strong, she needs an outlet for her excessive metal energy. Her favourable elements are water and wood, which help to exhaust the metal energy. Her unfavourable element is earth which is already excessive in her destiny. Another enemy which can upset her balance is fire as fire generates stronger earth. With this hypothesis, a compatible marriage partner is thus a man with the water and wood elements in his destiny to meet her needs.

Let us now look at the birth data of Mr O. J. Simpson to see if he is a suitable candidate.

HOUR	DAY	MONTH	YEAR
戊 Earth	己 Earth	丁 Fire	丁 Fire
辰 Earth	丑 Earth	未 Earth	亥 Water

60	50	40	30	20	10	0
庚 Metal	辛 Metal	壬 Water	癸 Water	甲 Wood	乙 Wood	丙 Fire
子 Water	丑 Earth	寅 Wood	卯 Wood	辰 Earth	巳 Fire	午 Fire

The Pillars of Destiny of Mr O. J. Simpson

Mr Simpson is a man of earth. He was born in a summer month when the strong fire provides strong support to the earth element. He is thus a strong earth person who needs an outlet for his excessive earth energy. His favourable elements are metal and water. Metal represents his skill, intelligence and aspirations while water is his symbol for money. Wood too is quite favourable as it conquers earth and keeps his excessive earth element under control. The other two elements, fire and earth, are his enemies as they generate a stronger earth element, creating even more imbalance for his Four Pillars of Destiny.

In the previous chapters, we have learned that a basic requirement for a close relationship is that one party must possess the favourable element of the other party. As Ms Brown's favourable elements are water and wood, we would expect to find plenty of water and wood elements in Mr Simpson's destiny. But there is hardly any water and wood in his birth data. So how do we explain the attraction between these two persons that developed into a marriage relationship?

The birth data is not the only influence in our destiny. One other major factor that greatly impacts our lives is our luck pillars. The luck pillars are derived from the month pillar and symbolise the cyclical changes of life. Each luck pillar governs a period of ten years of our lives and represents a pair of elements which cast considerable influence on our destiny during the ten year period. The luck pillars represent our passage through life. We can make a simple analogy in this manner. The Four Pillars are like a car that sets out on a journey. The luck pillars are the road on which the car of destiny will travel. To complete the journey successfully, you need a good car as well as a good road. If the road is rough and full of obstacles, no matter how good your car is, it will not be able to travel smoothly. Hence the impact of the luck pillars is as important as the Four Pillars of Destiny.

If we examine Mr Simpson's luck pillars, we can explain his success as a football star and movie actor. The month pillar represents his parents and hence his background. It is occupied by the unfavourable elements of fire and earth. Mr Simpson does not come from a well-off family and his parents could offer little help in his career. His luck pillars also show a passage of strong fire influences during the first 20 years of his life. As fire is unfavourable, it shows that he did not live in comfort during his childhood and youth. It was not until the third luck pillar – one of wood over earth – that he encountered his favourable elements in life.

O. J. Simpson's Rise to Fame

Looking at the success story of Mr Simpson, we can see that this timing of events matches very well with his family background and childhood. He was born of a poor family and his father left his mother when he was four years old. His mother had to shoulder the heavy burden of raising four children alone by working in a hospital. During childhood, Mr Simpson suffered bone deformation due to a poor diet. He did not do well in school and was arrested several times during his teens for minor offences such as fighting and stealing. But better luck found him when he began showing his athletic abilities as he approached the age of 20. He became an excellent football player in college and won scholarships for his outstanding sports performances. In 1968, when he turned 21, he was named 'Outstanding College Player of the 1960s' and collected a number of NCAA running records.

Mr Simpson's football career really took off in 1969, a year of metal which provided a strong outlet for his excessive earth energy. That year, he joined the Buffalo Bills as a professional football player. In September the same year, ABC Sports signed him on a long-term broadcasting contract and he became a national TV and radio personality. The subsequent five years from 1970 to 1975 were all years of favourable metal, water and wood. Mr Simpson emerged as one of the most well-liked athletes in America. His career peaked in 1975, a year of strong wood, when he was named first runner-up in the *Sports Illustrated* Sportsman of the Year Award.

Mr Simpson's fame and fortune continued into his very favourable luck pillar of water and wood after he turned 30. He became a popular movie star, starring in several successful movies in the 1970s.

From Mr Simpson's early history we can established that the elements of water, wood and metal brought him good luck while earth and fire brought him misfortunes. This hypothesis offers an explanation for his ups and downs in life and provides an insight into his marriage life.

Mr Simpson met Ms Nicole Brown in June 1977 and they began dating immediately. Such instant attraction is usually the result of complementary elements, where the destiny of each party possesses the element that the other party needs. Ms Brown is a strong metal lady whose metal symbolises the outlet Mr Simpson needs for his excessive earth energy. This explains why Mr Simpson fell in love with Ms Brown at first sight.

What about Ms Brown? From our analysis, we concluded that she needs water and wood as her favourable elements but these are not available in Mr Simpson's destiny. However, in 1977, Mr Simpson had turned 30 and had stepped into a luck pillar of strong water and wood. This luck pillar provided the wood and water that attracted Ms Brown. When Ms Brown met Mr Simpson in 1977, she was only 18 years old and was in a luck pillar of strong metal and earth. The pressure created by the excessive metal left her badly in need of an outlet in the form of water and wood.

Their love affair developed dramatically and they eventually got married in 1985. Ms Brown gave birth to two children – one in 1985 and another in 1988.

According to several biographies of Mr Simpson, tension then began to creep into their marriage. On New Year's Day 1989, the police were called to their home and Mr Simpson was arrested for assaulting his wife. In October 1993, Ms Brown called the police again after she was beaten by her husband. Mr Simpson was charged with spouse abuse and was later sentenced to 120 hours of community service and two years probation.

What Triggered the Downturn?

How can we explain this drastic deterioration in their relationship? It is not uncommon for couples to experience a change in feelings towards their partners after a certain time. Most of us have had the same experience. Someone you had found very attractive and compatible yesterday may not be equally attractive today. The loving feeling may seem to have totally disappeared. Social scientists and psychologists can offer many explanations for this phenomenon. But from the metaphysical point of view, the reason is quite simple. Our change in needs and what we like are all governed by the change of elemental influences in our destiny.

In our analysis, we have explained that Mr Simpson needed Ms Brown's metal element while Ms Brown needed Mr Simpson's water and wood elements. These are the elements which caused instant attraction. These same elements are responsible for maintaining the attraction and keeping their relationship intact. But when we grow older, we move from one luck pillar to another. When our luck pillars change, the elements we need also change. As we have seen, Ms Brown needed water and wood which is not found in Mr Simpson's destiny, but only in his luck pillar. This luck pillar only lasts ten years. When this luck pillar expires, the attraction is gone. And that is what happened when Mr Simpson turned 40 in 1987.

At 40, Mr Simpson moved into another luck pillar of water and wood. This luck pillar, though similar to the previous luck pillar of water and wood, is symbolised by a different set of Chinese characters – yang water and wood, as opposed to the previous yin water and wood. This difference is crucial.

In the last chapter, we examined the 'clash relationship' between two earthly branches. Clash implies conflict. There is however a more harmonious kind of relationship called 'combine'. In this relationship, when two heavenly stems or earthly branches meet, they are attracted to combine with one another. The following table shows the pairs of heavenly stems and earthly branches that can combine.

The combine relationships of the earthly branches

甲 (Yang Wood)	—	己 (Yin Earth)	
丙 (Yang Fire)	—	辛 (Yin Metal)	
戊 (Yang Earth)	—	癸 (Yin Water)	
庚 (Yang Metal)	—	乙 (Yin Wood)	
壬 (Yang Water)	—	丁 (Yin Fire)	

The combine relationships of the heavenly stems

A combine relationship is a harmonious one but it changes the nature of the element. For example, when the yang water heavenly stem combines with the yin fire heavenly stem, the water may lose its water nature. Similarly for the fire element. This is exactly what happened to Mr Simpson. The water and wood elements in his luck pillar of age 30 to 40 were energetic but when he turned 40, the new luck pillar of water and wood could not offer him the same lively water and wood. This is because yang water had combined with his two yin fire elements in the heavenly stem of his destiny, and the wood in his luck pillar had combined with the water earthly branch of his year pillar. The unfortunate result: his water is no longer water and his wood no longer wood. Water and wood are the main attraction for Ms Brown in the relationship. When these elements disappeared, the marriage broke down.

Nonetheless Mr Simpson was still strongly attracted to Ms Brown as the metal remained strong in her destiny. It was thus Ms Brown who filed for divorce. Mr Simpson was very much against it and he launched a determined effort to win her back.

Up to this point, readers will be able to appreciate how our shifting luck pillars can change our feelings and our elemental needs. It is these changes that are usually responsible for turning a good marriage sour.

Another important step, as we have discussed earlier, is to examine the House of Spouse, which is found in the earthly branch of a person's day pillar. In Mr Simpson's destiny, his day pillar is earth over earth. As earth is unfavourable to him, this is a sign that his marriage life will not be happy. Mr Simpson divorced his first wife in 1979, a year of strong earth with the year earthly branch (goat) clashing with his House of Spouse (ox). This clash is a strong indication of trouble in marriage. For Ms Brown, her day pillar is metal on earth. Her House of Spouse is thus earth, also an unfavourable element for her, indicating that her marriage life too will not be successful. Earth, by nature, supports metal. But when it becomes excessive, its negative meaning is that of an overly attentive and possessive spouse who restricts the self's freedom. Perhaps this is why Ms Brown wanted out from the marriage in 1992.

The O. J. Simpson story will not be complete without a brief mention of his controversial murder trial and civil damage trial. He was acquitted of murder in the first trial in 1995 but was convicted in the civil damage trial in 1997. I still remember a conversation with the Chairman of the International Council of Shopping Centres during the council's annual convention in Singapore in 1995, one day before the verdict in Mr Simpson's murder trial. The Chairman asked me to predict the verdict. My answer was, 'If his birth data is correct, I think he will go free.' He announced this to the convention immediately!

It is not difficult to make such a prediction if you know how to use the technique of the Four Pillars of Destiny. As we know, Mr Simpson's favourable elements are water and wood. As long as he is under the influence of these elements, it will not be possible to convict him. 1996 was a year of strong water, so Mr Simpson would not be greeting that year from a jail cell. 1997, however, was a year of fire and earth, his most unfavourable elements. That was why he lost his battle against the civil charges in 1997.

Flowers of Romance

The 10 heavenly stems and 12 earthly branches were known to exist in the Chinese calendar as far back as the Hsia dynasty more than 6,000 years ago. So the origin of this system is not clear. The heavenly stems refer to elemental influences from heaven (the cosmos beyond the earth). The 12 earthly branches, by their name, imply elemental influences of the earth. The 12 earthly branches also represent the 12 months of a year and the 24 hours in a day. They reflect the cyclical change of the five elements through time. The 12 months of a year represent seasonal cycles of the earth due to the changing position of the sun in relation to the earth, brought about by the movement of the earth round the sun. The 24 hours of a day represent the changing position of the earth caused by the self rotation of the earth.

The earthly branches can also be understood as the 12 equal divisions of the circle called the ecliptic, which represents the different positions of the sun in relation to the earth. This is similar to the zodiac signs of astrology. Hence the 12 earthly branches carry meanings related to the five elements and their seasonal changes with time and space. They reflect the life cycle of the elements in a year. Wood is strongest in spring, fire is most prosperous in summer, metal is the prevailing influence in autumn and water is the ruling element in winter. The remaining element earth is so basic and important that it is present all year round. On basis of this principle, we can look at the 12 earthly branches in terms of the 12 months representing the four seasons of a year:

Hsia Months		Element	Season	Western Months
1	寅	Wood	Spring	4, 5 Feb – 5, 6 Mar
2	卯	Wood	Spring	5, 6 Mar – 4, 5 Apr
3	辰	Earth	Spring	4, 5 Apr – 5, 6 May
4	巳	Fire	Summer	5, 6 May – 5, 6 June
5	午	Fire	Summer	5, 6 June – 7, 8 July
6	未	Earth	Summer	7, 8 July – 7, 8 Aug
7	申	Metal	Autumn	7, 8 Aug – 7, 8 Sep
8	酉	Metal	Autumn	7, 8 Sep – 8, 9 Oct
9	戌	Earth	Autumn	8, 9 Oct – 7, 8 Nov
10	亥	Water	Winter	7, 8 Nov – 7, 8 Dec
11	子	Water	Winter	7, 8 Dec – 5, 6 Jan
12	丑	Earth	Winter	5, 6 Jan – 4, 5 Feb

The relationship between the Hsia calendar and the Western calendar

In the Hsia calendar (the calendar using heavenly stems and earthly branches), a year starts on the date called 'arrival of spring', which normally falls on 4 or 5 February of the Western calendar. From the above table, we can see that the first two months of the year, equivalent to February and March, are symbolised by wood earthly branches, as wood is the dominating element in spring. If we divide a year equally into four seasons, each season will consist of three months. The first two months are represented by the dominating element of the season while the third month is represented by the earth element, symbolising that the earth influence prevails all year round.

The second month of each season is the month when the dominating element is strongest. The strongest wood is found in March, the strongest fire in June, the strongest metal in September, and the most prosperous water in December.

The earthly branches representing the strongest wood, fire, metal and water have many implications when we interpret a set of Four Pillars of Destiny. One of the important implications is that they are the 'Flowers of Romance'.

The origin of this concept is rather complicated. Basically, each element, when passing through the year, undergoes a complete cycle of growth, comparable to a newborn baby going through 12 stages of growing up, maturing, prospering and finally deteriorating. Take the wood element as an example. The life cycle of wood starts in November. It begins to grow as a child in December, goes to school in January, graduates in February, becomes mature and strong in March, then begins to decay in April, falls sick in May, starts deteriorating in June, and enters the death bed in July, with life terminating in August. Inception takes place again in September, with preparations to germinate in October. Hence one full cycle is completed in 12 months. In this cycle, the month to note is December. For the wood element, the proper term to describe this month, symbolising a baby growing up, is 'taking a bath'. This term is related to obscenity. Hence the earthly branch representing December is called a 'Flower of Romance'. Using the same method, we can also derive the other 'Flowers of Romance' by bringing the other elements through their full 12-stage life cycle and determining the month when they 'take a bath'.

The following table lists the 'Flowers of Romance':

Flower of Romance	Applicable to Year of Birth or Date of Birth		
Rat（子）	Pig（亥）	Rabbit（卯）	Goat（未）
Horse（午）	Snake（巳）	Rooster（酉）	Ox（丑）
Rabbit（卯）	Tiger（寅）	Horse（午）	Dog（戌）
Rooster（酉）	Monkey（申）	Rat（子）	Dragon（辰）

The 'Flowers of Romance'

Emperor Chien Lung: Super Lover

If many Flowers of Romance are found in a person's destiny, it could mean he is very attractive to the opposite sex or that he has many chances to encounter the opposite sex and develop relationships. A famous example in Chinese history is Emperor Chien Lung of the Ching dynasty. His Four Pillars of Destiny are shown here:

HOUR	DAY	MONTH	YEAR
丙 Fire	庚 Metal	丁 Fire	辛 Metal
子 Water	午 Fire	酉 Metal	卯 Wood

The Four Pillars of Emperor Chien Lung of the Ching Dynasty

Emperor Chien Lung possessed all four Flowers of Romance in the earthly branches of his four pillars. He enjoyed a great reputation with women and had numerous romances during his reign.

Hugh Grant's Midnight Encounter

Let us also examine the following more contemporary example:

HOUR	DAY	MONTH	YEAR
?	庚 Metal	乙 Wood	庚 Metal
?	子 Water	酉 Metal	子 Water

70	60	50	40	30	20	10
壬 Water	辛 Metal	庚 Metal	己 Earth	戊 Earth	丁 Fire	丙 Fire
辰 Earth	卯 Wood	寅 Wood	丑 Earth	子 Water	亥 Water	戌 Earth

The Pillars of Destiny of Mr Hugh Grant

This set of Four Pillars of Destiny belongs to the famous British actor Mr Hugh Grant. Born on a day of metal in autumn when metal dominates, he is a strong metal man. Water and wood are his favourable elements that help exhaust the metal. Metal and earth are unfavourable as they increase the strength of metal and unbalance his Four Pillars.

Water symbolises his talents and skill while wood symbolises his money. He possesses two water elements in his year and day pillars. Moreover, after the age of 30, he entered a luck pillar of strong water. These powerful water elements helped made him a popular international movie star, especially in the strong water and wood years between 1992 and 1996.

Now let us examine his romance aspects. Immediately we are struck by the strong resemblance between Mr Hugh Grant and Emperor Chien Lung. Both are metal men born in the same month of metal. In Hugh Grant's destiny, his three known earthly branches are Rat, Rooster and Rat – all Flowers of Romance. Like the earlier example of Emperor Chien Lung, this explains his attractiveness to the opposite sex. Checking the nature of his Flowers of Romance against the earlier table, we find that as Mr Grant is a Rat, the Rooster in his month pillar is his true Romance Flower. Above this Rooster is an element of wood on the heavenly stem. For a metal man, wood is the symbol of female friends. Hence this month pillar of wood over Rooster represents a beautiful woman who has a romance with Mr Grant. This woman is however surrounded by two metal elements, one in the day pillar, symbolising Mr Grant himself, the other in the year pillar, symbolising another man, a competitor to Mr Grant.

This configuration shows that despite Mr Grant's attractiveness to women, he faces strong competition in romance. Another possible interpretation is that he may encounter an attractive woman who is not fully devoted to him. He has to share the woman with other man. A prostitute fits the description of such a woman.

In 1995, Mr Grant had an embarrassing experience. In the early hours of 27 June, he was caught by a police officer in Hollywood's Sunset Boulevard and was charged together with prostitute Ms Divine Brown with 'lewd conduct' in his car. How is this incident reflected in Mr Grant's Pillars of Destiny?

The year 1995 was a year of wood on water. This was a good year for Mr Grant as wood is money and water his opportunity to display his talents. At the age of 35 he was into a luck pillar of water. The strong water is his intelligence element, representing creativity and talent. But if excessive, the water also represents over-aggressiveness and rebellion. This is the element that drives our desire to rebel against social restrictions. So it was not surprising that Mr Grant was in the mood to seek some pleasure on the night of 26 June and the early morning of 27 June. The time of the incident is represented below:

HOUR	DAY	MONTH	YEAR
甲 Wood	戊 Earth	壬 Water	乙 Wood
子 Water	子 Water	午 Fire	庚 Water

26 June 1995, midnight – when Mr Hugh Grant encountered Ms Divine Brown

53

HOUR	DAY	MONTH	YEAR
乙	己	壬	乙
Wood	Earth	Water	Wood
丑	丑	午	亥
Earth	Earth	Fire	Water

27 June 1995, early morning – when Mr Grant was caught by the police

At midnight, 26 June, four water elements appear in the four pillars. The strong water is favourable and Mr Grant is in a happy mood. But the water also stimulates his aggression. Under such influence it is difficult to exercise self restraint, which is symbolised by the fire element in the month pillar. The fire is suppressed by water, so he is tempted to do something unconventional. The wood element symbolises a woman to a metal man and wood appears in both the year and the hour pillars – signalling the appearance of Ms Divine Brown. The yin wood in the year pillar is instantly attracted to the yang metal of Mr Grant, as shown in the 'combine' relationships of heavenly stems in the last chapter.

A New Day and a Very Different Configuration

The early morning of 27 June shows a very different configuration of pillars. The day is now a day of earth and the morning hour of one a.m. an hour of wood on earth. There are three earth elements supported by the fire element in the month pillar. Earth is unfavourable so Mr Grant encounters some misfortune. The fire element is destructive to metal; although it symbolises status and power, in the negative sense, it also represents discipline and the law – in other words, the policeman.

The fire is in the month pillar so its influence is quite strong. As 27 June dawns, the fire is no longer suppressed by water and has become a significant influence. Hence the appearance of the police. The impact of fire is that it stimulates and supports the earth element which spells misfortune in Mr Grant's destiny. Earth is the resource element to a metal person, but when excessive, it suppresses water, restricts freedom of expression and makes the person feel suffocated and frustrated. This must have been exactly how Mr Grant must have felt when he was caught by the police with Ms Divine Brown in his car.

Another interesting aspect can be observed from the destiny of Ms Brown. Born on 8 August 1969, Ms Brown's destiny is shown below:

HOUR	DAY	MONTH	YEAR
?	乙 Wood	辛 Metal	己 Earth
?	卯 Wood	未 Earth	酉 Metal

50	40	30	20	10	0
丁 Fire	丙 Fire	乙 Wood	甲 Wood	癸 Water	壬 Water
丑 Earth	子 Water	亥 Water	戌 Earth	酉 Metal	申 Metal

The Pillars of Destiny of Ms Divine Brown

Ms Brown was born on a day of yin wood. From the table showing the combine relationships among the heavenly stems, we can see that this yin wood combines with the yang metal of Hugh Grant.

Most of us will have observed that there are people whom we can get along with better than others. I have explained in a previous chapter that this may be because the other person possesses plenty of our favourable elements. However, there could be another equally important factor at play – the combine relationship between the heavenly stems of our day pillars. If we check the table showing the combine aspects of the heavenly stems, we will see that yin wood combines with yang metal. Ms Brown is a yin wood lady and Mr Grant is a yang metal man. So the two day pillars combine, creating instant attraction. Mr Grant thus cannot resist the charms of Ms Brown in the small hours between 26 June and 27 June.

This incident demonstrates how we can apply the Flowers of Romance to detect our chances of encountering the opposite sex. By using the table above, we can derive our relevant Flower of Romance in accordance with the earthly branches of the year pillar or day pillar. After identifying the relevant Flower of Romance, we can then watch out for that particular year, month or day to look for romance.

However, bear in mind that a Flower of Romance is not always positive. If the Flower is also one's favourable element then it may help one get married. But if it is an unfavourable element, it may bring scandal. In our example of Hugh Grant, Mr Grant's Flower of Romance is the Rooster, an unfavourable metal element that brought misfortune when he encountered Ms Brown. For those of us who are married, such a Flower of Romance can be particularly dangerous when it clashes with the day pillar – the House of Spouse. Often, such a clash is a sign of trouble in family life …

Matchmaking, the Old-Fashioned Way

Animal sign astrology is perhaps the area in Chinese metaphysics that generates the most interest. Unfortunately it is also the cause of considerable misunderstanding.

The 12 animal signs – Rat, Ox, Tiger, Rabbit, Dragon, Snake, Horse, Goat, Monkey, Rooster, Dog and Pig – refer to our years of birth. In the Chinese calendar as well as the system of Four Pillars of Destiny, the 12 animal signs are represented by the 12 earthly branches of a 12-year cycle. There is much literature available on animal signs. Like Western astrology, people born under different animal signs are said to possess different types of personality. In most cases, this personality is related to the characteristics of the animal. At the beginning of each year, many booklets are published, predicting the fortunes of people born under each animal sign.

Now, anyone who has a fair understanding of the Chinese calendar and the Four Pillars of Destiny will realise that the so-called 'animal sign astrology' is as illogical as newspaper astrology in the West. As we have seen, we need to know the Four Pillars – year, month, day and hour – before we can carry out any meaningful destiny analysis. The animal signs only refer to the earthly branches of the year pillar, thus providing only one-eighth of the required information. Its influence on our destiny is very limited. Moreover, it is preposterous to believe that the entire human population has only 12 types of fate!

Even so, the animal signs have a deep-rooted tradition in Chinese culture and have traditionally been adopted by the layman for marriage matching. Certain animal signs, it is believed, should not get married because they clash with each other.

This type of marriage matching actually originates from the clash and combine relationships between the earthly branches that we have discussed earlier. The following tables show the clash and combine relationships among the earthly branches, or animal signs:

子 Rat	—	午 Horse
丑 Ox	—	未 Goat
寅 Tiger	—	申 Monkey
卯 Rabbit	—	酉 Rooster
辰 Dragon	—	戌 Dog
巳 Snake	—	亥 Pig

Animal signs in clash relationships

子 Rat	—	丑 Ox
寅 Tiger	—	亥 Pig
辰 Dragon	—	酉 Rooster
午 Horse	—	未 Goat
申 Monkey	—	巳 Snake
戌 Dog	—	卯 Rabbit

Animal signs in combine relationships

申 Monkey	+	子 Rat	+	辰 Dragon	=	Water combination
亥 Pig	+	卯 Rabbit	+	未 Goat	=	Wood combination
巳 Snake	+	酉 Rooster	+	丑 Ox	=	Metal combination
寅 Tiger	+	午 Horse	+	戌 Dog	=	Fire combination

Three animal signs in combine relationships

For example, if you were born in the year of the Rat, you would be in clash with a person born in the year of the Horse. You will be advised not to marry a Horse person. Such clashes always occur when two persons are six years apart in their ages. But a Rat can combine with an Ox, a Monkey or a Dragon, so these animal signs are considered good marriage partners for a Rat.

How valid is this system? As explained previously, the full set of Four Pillars of Destiny must be analysed to determine each person's favourable elements before we can comment on compatibility. So it is quite wrong to deny a couple their chance to marry merely because the animal signs of their birth years clash. In the past, when marriages were dictated and pre-arranged by the parents, this system of marriage matching did not cause much hardship as the boy and the girl did not even know each other when their birth data were compared. However, the situation is quite different today. People fall in love before they consider marriage. So this erroneous concept of marriage matching by animal signs should not be allowed to create unnecessary obstacles for lovers.

Today, the technique of the Four Pillars of Destiny can still be used to help in marriage matching. We can assess compatibility between two persons by checking whether each possesses the favourable elements of the other partner. We can also see if there are any combine relationships in the day pillar which add to the mutual attraction. And we can look into the future prospects of the marriage relationship. This matching exercise, however, should be done well before a couple has fallen deeply in love. In practice, if a couple has already decided to get married, I would usually suggest that they just select an auspicious date for the happy event and discourage them from going through the marriage matching exercise as it would be very disappointing if the result turns out to be negative. The tool of marriage matching should best be applied when a lady has a few admirers and wishes to choose one as the marriage candidate.

Three Men and A Lady

Let me demonstrate this technique with a real-life example:

HOUR	DAY	MONTH	YEAR
丙 Fire	丁 Fire	戊 Earth	甲 Wood
午 Fire	亥 Water	辰 Earth	辰 Earth

59	49	39	29	19	9
壬 Water	癸 Water	甲 Wood	乙 Wood	丙 Fire	丁 Fire
戊 Earth	亥 Water	子 Water	丑 Earth	寅 Wood	卯 Wood

The Pillars of Destiny of a lady client

These Four Pillars of Destiny belong to a pretty, intelligent and wealthy lady who was looking for a suitable husband when she consulted me. She is a lady of fire born with a considerable amount of earth elements. As fire gives birth to earth, the earth is exhausting her fire energy. Her fire needs the support of wood, which in turn needs support of water. Her favourable elements are thus wood and water. Earth and metal, which further weaken the fire, are unfavourable elements.

Earth is a symbol of intelligence, so this lady is capable and wise. However, earth suppresses water, the symbol of her male partner and husband. The excessive amount of earth thus creates an obstacle to her marriage – her intelligence is curtailing her chance to encounter a good husband. This phenomenon is common in modern society: it is a social norm for a lady to find a husband more capable than herself, but if the lady herself is intelligent and successful in her career, her pool of suitable candidates is naturally much smaller as there are fewer men who are superior to her in ability. This lady faced such a problem. She had many male admirers but most did not possess the social status or ability to match her success.

When she came to consult me, she was 30 years old. Her first question was, "Will I ever get married?" The husband's element in her destiny is water, and this water is found in her House of Spouse, thus signifying that she will have a husband. However, the water is weak as it is suppressed by the strong earth elements in the year and the month pillars. The year and the month pillars symbolise her family background and her parents. So it appears her intelligence is not the only obstacle to her marriage. Her parents and family background are also a contributory factor. Sure enough, this lady is from a very wealthy and reputable family who naturally demand a son-in-law of comparable status.

Her luck pillars show that she went through good periods of strong wood and fire during childhood which provided her with comfort and a good education. But these luck pillars did not help her water. And no water element appears in her luck pillars before the age of 39. We can conclude that her chance of getting married certainly exists but it will come later in life. The water element – symbolising her husband – has been weak so far. She will have to wait for a period when the water becomes strong. This luck pillar will only appear at the age of 39. However, it does not mean that no meaningful romance will occur before the age of 39. Male partners will still appear during a year of strong water. So in water years such as 1992, 1993 and 1996 she had many admirers. When she came to me, she provided the birth data of several of these candidates:

HOUR	DAY	MONTH	YEAR
乙 Wood	戊 Earth	戊 Earth	乙 Wood
卯 Wood	申 Metal	寅 Wood	酉 Metal

61	51	41	31	21	11	1
辛 Metal	壬 Water	癸 Water	甲 Wood	乙 Wood	丙 Fire	丁 Fire
未 Earth	申 Metal	酉 Metal	戌 Earth	亥 Water	子 Water	丑 Earth

Gentleman A (born 1945)

HOUR	DAY	MONTH	YEAR
辛 Metal	乙 Wood	壬 Water	乙 Wood
巳 Fire	巳 Fire	午 Fire	巳 Fire

65	55	45	35	25	15	5
乙 Wood	丙 Fire	丁 Fire	戊 Earth	己 Earth	庚 Metal	辛 Metal
亥 Water	子 Water	丑 Earth	寅 Wood	卯 Wood	辰 Earth	巳 Fire

Gentleman B (born 1965)

HOUR	DAY	MONTH	YEAR
戊 Earth	庚 Metal	丁 Fire	癸 Water
寅 Wood	辰 Earth	巳 Fire	卯 Wood

60	50	40	30	20	10
辛 Metal	壬 Water	癸 Water	甲 Wood	乙 Wood	丙 Fire
亥 Water	子 Water	丑 Earth	寅 Wood	卯 Wood	辰 Earth

Gentleman C (born 1963)

These three candidates should be examined on the basis of the following criteria:

a. As the lady's favourable element is wood, a suitable candidate should possess sufficient wood elements in his Four Pillars. This will ensure compatibility in elemental needs so that the lady will at least be attracted to the man.

b. The lady's Four Pillars possess strong earth elements, so to ensure that there is genuine mutual attraction between the man and the lady, the Four Pillars of the candidate should show that earth is his favourable element.

c. The candidate's Four Pillars should indicate he is into reasonably good fortune and such favourable fortune should be long lasting. Your objective is to help your client achieve a happy and lasting marriage. You should at least caution your client if a candidate is expected to encounter some misfortunes in the near future.

d. As your client is a capable and successful lady, this should be reflected in the candidate's Four Pillars. In other words, the candidate's element representing the spouse, or the House of Spouse, must be reasonably strong.

e. The candidate's Four Pillars should reflect a harmonious relationship with his future wife.

f. The candidate should be reasonably qualified in terms of education, status and financial standing, and should be reasonably successful in his career.

g. If your client is eager to get married as soon as possible, the candidate's Four Pillars should reflect that he has the opportunity to get married in the near future.

Your topmost concern is the future wellbeing of your client so you must examine all aspects thoroughly and not miss any pitfalls which may lead to problems in her future marriage. Applying all these criteria to the three candidates, the one born in 1963 appears to have the highest score. He is a metal man born in summer with strong wood and fire elements.

To a metal person, wood is money and fire is status. Being a weak metal person, his favourable element is earth which occupies his House of Spouse. This is a good sign, indicating that he will have a supportive wife. His month pillar of fire is a symbol of his parents. Fire gives birth to earth in the House of Spouse, showing that his parents will be in harmony with his wife. This is also an important aspect to ensure harmony in family life.

At the time of consultation in 1993, this man was 31 years old and in a luck pillar of wood, an unfavourable element. This was reflected in his not-too-successful career thus far. His favourable element earth would arrive only after the age of 40 in his next luck pillar. So if money was not of paramount importance to my lady client, this gentleman was a good candidate.

A metal man, wood represents his wife. So a strong presence of wood would indicate his chance to get married. He was in a luck pillar of strong wood, and with the forthcoming 1995 being a year of yin wood, he could be expected to encounter strong romance in 1995. The subsequent years of 1997 to 2000 are all strong earth years, inviting good luck and success in both career and relationships.

However, we still have to examine the other two candidates before jumping to any conclusion. Both these candidates also possess strong wood elements but they have more drawbacks.

Gentleman A (born 1945) is a weak earth person and needs the support of fire. He was 49 years old in 1994 and in a luck pillar of water and metal, unfavourable elements which exhaust his weak earth energy. He faces another 10 years of bad luck.

Gentleman B (born 1965) is a man of wood with strong fire. As the wood is being exhausted by fire, his favourable elements are water and wood. He is in a good luck pillar of wood so his career is successful. However, he needs water and wood, both of which do not feature prominently in my lady client's Four Pillars. Instead, her strong earth element is unfavourable to him. Moreover too much fire carries the negative implication of aggressiveness to the point of being rebellious. His resource element water, representing conservatism, education, and self-restraint, is also totally lacking. This man is too aggressive and lacks discipline (metal) and restraint (water). He is not as stable as candidate C.

In conclusion, all three men have drawbacks but Mr C appears to be a more reliable choice.

Troubled Relationships

The controversy surrounding the break-up of the romance between Hollywood personalities Mia Farrow and Woody Allen provides a good case study for us to examine how a love relationship can deteriorate into a legal battle.

HOUR	DAY	MONTH	YEAR
?	辛 Metal	丁 Fire	乙 Wood
?	亥 Water	亥 Water	亥 Water

68	58	48	38	28	18	8
庚 Metal	辛 Metal	壬 Water	癸 Water	甲 Wood	乙 Wood	丙 Fire
辰 Earth	巳 Fire	午 Fire	未 Earth	申 Metal	酉 Metal	戌 Earth

The Pillars of Destiny of Mr Woody Allen (1/12/35)

Mr Woody Allen is a metal man born in the winter month when water is most prosperous. He possesses plenty of water, which symbolises his creative skill in acting and movie directing, in his Four Pillars, but these water elements also exhaust his metal, making him weak. He needs more metal elements as well as support from earth. Fire which supports earth is also favourable. Water and wood will weaken him. Remembering our rule that a compatible partner must possess one's favourable element, we can expect Ms Mia Farrow, with whom Mr Allen fell in love around 1979, to possess the required fire and earth in her destiny.

Let us now examine Ms Farrow's Four Pillars. Ms Farrow was born on 9 February 1945. Converting her birth data into the Chinese calendar, her Four Pillars of Destiny are as follows:

HOUR	DAY	MONTH	YEAR
庚 Metal	己 Earth	戊 Earth	乙 Wood
午 Fire	酉 Metal	寅 Wood	酉 Metal

59	49	39	29	19	9
甲 Wood	癸 Water	壬 Water	辛 Metal	庚 Metal	己 Earth
申 Metal	未 Earth	午 Fire	巳 Fire	辰 Earth	卯 Wood

The Pillars of Destiny of Ms Mia Farrow (9/2/45)

She is an earth lady born in the spring month of wood. She possesses plenty of metal which is a symbol of her creativity and intelligence in acting. She also possesses fire in her hour pillar and this fire is well supported by the strong wood in spring. Hence she possesses plenty of earth, fire and metal, exactly the elements Mr Allen needs. This explains why Mr Allen was very much attracted to her when they became friends in 1979.

But as an earth lady born in a wood month, Ms Farrow's earth is not strong. Wood conquers earth so she needs more fire to support her earth. Her favourable elements are fire and earth. Unfavourable elements are metal and water which exhaust her earth strength.

You may however be puzzled to find no earth element but plenty of metal and water, which are unfavourable to Ms Farrow, in Mr Allen's destiny. Love affairs are not a one-sided business. Romance can only be stimulated if Mr Allen was also able to provide Ms Farrow with her favourable elements – fire and earth. So how can we explain their falling in love in 1979?

The key is in Ms Farrow's luck pillars. In 1979, at the age of 34, Ms Farrow was in a luck pillar of fire. Fire provides strong support to her earth element so she was not a weak earth lady at that time. As 1979 was also a year of strong fire and earth, these multiple fire and earth elements helped transform Ms Farrow into a strong earth lady. Instead of finding metal and water exhaustive, she now needed these elements as an outlet for her excessive earth energy! This example shows that one's favourable elements can change with time according to the influence of our luck pillars. Under such circumstance of strong fire and earth, Ms Farrow fell in love with Mr Allen's metal and water elements.

Now, if a love affair can be brought about purely by the influence of a particular luck pillar, it is logical to expect that such a relationship can change after the luck pillar responsible for such a love affair expires. The relationship between Ms Farrow and Mr Allen very much depends on the presence of the strong fire element found in Ms Farrow's luck pillars between the age of 34 and 49. The strong fire increased the strength of Ms Farrow's earth self and enabled her to withstand the exhaustive metal and water elements so abundant in Mr Allen's destiny. But once the fire weakens, Ms Farrow's earth will become weak again and metal and water will become too exhaustive for her. When this happens, the attraction between Ms Farrow and Mr Allen will fade and their relationship will deteriorate.

From Mr Allen's point of view, the fire element is equally important for him to maintain a good relationship with Ms Farrow. Mr Allen is weak metal man who needs the support of earth and fire. He will be attracted to Ms Farrow only as long as she possesses plenty of strong earth and fire in her destiny. Once the fire and earth in Ms Farrow's destiny diminishes, the relationship will fall apart.

The Break-up

According to reports, Ms Farrow and Mr Allen maintained an excellent relationship from 1979 till around 1990. Things then turned bad from late 1991/early 1992 when Ms Farrow discovered that Mr Allen was having an affair with one of her adopted daughters, Soon-Yi. In 1992, Ms Farrow was 47 and was still in her luck pillar of fire. How then can we explain the downturn in their good relationship? In the system of the Four Pillars of Destiny, we are not only under the influence of the elements in our destiny and luck pillars, but also very much affected by the elements brought about by each year, month, day and even hour. Since 1991, the yearly elemental influences have entered a strong metal and water cycle, with 1992 and 1993 being the years of strongest metal and water. So even though Ms Farrow was still in a luck pillar of fire, her fire and hence her earth, became quite weak after 1991, and so the metal and water elements became unfavourable to her. With the demise of the fire element after 1991, her relationship with Mr Allen turned sour. Mr Allen needed the support of fire and earth from Ms Farrow's destiny, so when her fire and earth weakened drastically, he turned to another lady as his new source of these elements.

Ms Farrow and Mr Allen's relationship deteriorated so badly that in 1993, they fought a legal battle for the custody of their adopted children.

This example illustrates how a couple's relationship hangs on the delicate balance of the elements in their destiny. The changing elements will unconsciously affect our mood and our feelings towards our loved ones. It can create critical moments in our relationship. With the changing elemental influence from year to year, month to month and day to day, disharmony can easily arise. If we do not exercise self restraint and just allow the elemental influence to take over our temperament, a passing bad mood may blow up into a serious quarrel or even destroy a long relationship.

By being aware of our destiny and the elemental influences on our lives, we can understand a situation better and exercise self restraint to overcome any anger brought on by our mood. We can be more tolerant of any apparent wrong doing by our loved ones, achieve a deeper understanding of the motives and reasons behind such wrong doings, and perhaps even forgive our partners more generously.

The key words to maintaining a long-lasting relationship are understanding, tolerance and forgiveness.

A Happy Ending

We have examined various aspects of love affairs and marriage relationships and have demonstrated how the elements in our destiny can create opportunities for us to meet our lovers, generate mutual attraction between two persons and then be responsible for a subsequent change in attitude that breaks up a marriage relationship.

To help reinforce what we have learned so far, let us summarise the major techniques into a few main points:

1.   In all analyses, first establish the person's favourable and unfavourable elements. Often, instant attraction can develop with someone whose destiny possesses plenty of our favourable elements. Compatibility between two persons usually means that both persons possess the favourable elements of the other person. These favourable elements are responsible for the bond between two persons.

2.   The House of Spouse, symbolised by the earthly branch of our day pillar, reflects our relationship with our spouse. For example, if the heavenly stem, representing the person himself, destroys the earthly branch of the day pillar, it means that the self has a tendency to dominate the spouse.

3.   Examine the element symbolising the husband or wife. To a male, the wife is the element that the self destroys. To a female, the husband is the element that conquers the self. A strong presence of such husband or wife elements in the destiny, luck pillar or year of marriage indicates a good chance for marriage.

4.   A change of attitude, mood or temperament towards our loved ones can occur when our luck pillars shift, changing our favourable elements. For example, if the self is weak fire, the favourable element is wood which supports the fire. A good partner is one with plenty of wood in his or her destiny. But if this weak fire person enters a luck pillar of strong wood, leaving him self-sufficient in wood, he no longer needs the wood elements from his partner's destiny. This can cool his relationship with his partner.

5.   Marriage matching with Flowers of Romance can help create stronger chances for encountering the opposite sex and generating romance.

6.   A relationship can also deteriorate if husband and wife have different favourable elements. If the husband needs fire and the wife needs water, in a fire year the husband will achieve success but the wife will suffer. This situation, if it persists, can cause disharmony and break up a good marriage.

Once we understand these elemental influences, we can foresee critical periods in our relationships and take precautions. For example, if we anticipate a critical year ahead where troubles may arise between husband and wife, such understanding allows us to control our temper and be more tolerant towards our loved ones to avoid unnecessary conflicts and disruptions. We may even have to live apart for a while and reunite after the critical year is over.

A Model Relationship: Ted Turner and Jane Fonda

Let us now look at a marriage with a happy ending. This is a model relationship where both husband and wife are equally successful in their careers and yet they have been able to maintain a very good relationship. This is the story of Mr Ted Turner and Ms Jane Fonda.

HOUR	DAY	MONTH	YEAR
乙 Wood	壬 Water	壬 Water	丁 Fire
巳 Fire	午 Fire	子 Water	丑 Earth

65	55	45	35	25	15	5
己 Earth	戊 Earth	丁 Fire	丙 Fire	乙 Wood	甲 Wood	癸 Water
未 Earth	午 Fire	巳 Fire	辰 Earth	卯 Wood	寅 Wood	丑 Earth

The Pillars of Destiny of Ms Jane Fonda

70

Ms Jane Fonda is a lady of strong water. She needs wood to release her excessive water energy. Her favourable elements are wood , fire and earth. Wood symbolises her talent and skill. Fire is her money, and earth is her power and status. Her luck pillars show that she has enjoyed the good fortune of strong wood, fire and earth since the age of 15. These favourable elements have propelled her to great heights in her movie career. During the 30 years of strong wood and fire luck pillars between age 15 and 45, she won the Academy Award for Best Actress twice – in 1971 and 1979.

To examine her marriage life, we must look at the element that represents her husband. This is earth, the destroyer of water. After the age of 35, she entered a series of luck pillars with strong fire, symbolising her money. But the strongest earth element – symbolising a strong and successful husband – appeared only in her luck pillar of age 55. Earth supported by fire is very strong earth, indicating that she has a chance to marry a 'heavyweight' whose status at least matches hers. She married media tycoon Mr Ted Turner, the head of CNN television network, in 1991 at the age of 54 as she was about to move into this strong luck pillar of earth over fire. Looking into the future, the earth influence will last until she is 75, symbolising that her husband will remain strong in her life for many years to come.

HOUR	DAY	MONTH	YEAR
庚 Metal	乙 Wood	癸 Water	戊 Earth
辰 Earth	卯 Wood	亥 Water	寅 Wood

67	57	47	37	27	17	7
庚 Metal	己 Earth	戊 Earth	丁 Fire	丙 Fire	乙 Wood	甲 Wood
午 Fire	巳 Fire	辰 Earth	卯 Wood	寅 Wood	丑 Earth	子 Water

The Pillars of Destiny of Mr Ted Turner

71

Mr Ted Turner is a man of wood. His wood is quite strong as it is supported by other wood in the year pillar and the water in the month pillar. Winter wood needs the warmth of the sun, so his favourable elements are fire and earth, which also act as an outlet for his strong wood energy. Looking at his luck pillars, Mr Turner has enjoyed the influence of his favourable fire and earth elements since the age of 27. Fire represents his skill and talents; earth represents his money. He had many opportunities to display his skill and intelligence in the 20 years of fire between the age of 27 and 47. Since the age of 47, he has encountered strong earth elements which have brought him much wealth. A wood man, his wife is symbolised by earth. Strong earth appears after the age of 47, indicating that he has the chance to marry a strong lady with the status to match his success. With the strong earth element prevailing between the age of 47 and 67, the wife will remain strong in his life until he is at least 67.

Their excellent relationship is also reflected in their respective House of Spouse in the day pillars of their destiny. Ms Fonda was born on a day of water on fire so her relationship with her husband is reflected in the water-fire configuration. As water destroys fire, it shows that she could dominate the home. This, however, is not a problem as she is presently in a luck pillar of strong earth and fire. Hence the fire in her House of Spouse is strong. Still this shows that her husband respects her very much and leaves much authority in her hands. Mr Ted Turner was born on a day of wood over wood. The heavenly stem and earthly branch are of the same element, showing that husband and wife are of equal status and will share the same ups and downs in life.

Exclusively for Ladies: Fashion, Beauty & Accessories

We have seen that the five basic elements – metal, water, wood, earth and fire – exist everywhere and affect every part of our lives. Unconsciously every one of us is guided and shaped by the laws of the five elements. Understanding the elements allows us to understand ourselves and our changes in mood, taste and style better. For example, have you ever wondered why you fell in love with green in 1995 but favoured black in 1996? And then moved on to brown and yellow in 1997? This is because fashion trends are collective expressions of the mood and taste of designers and the public. And such shifting moods and interests are led by the prevailing elements. For example, as 1995 is a year of wood on water, wood was the prevailing influence. Wood refers to nature and greenery so there was a shift of interest to green during 1995.

Choosing the Best Colours

The five elements are very much at play in our daily lives and are directly related to colours. The following table shows the five elements as expressed in colours:

Metal	—	white, gold, silver, shiny colours
Wood	—	green, blue, dark brown
Water	—	black, gray
Fire	—	red, purple, pink
Earth	—	yellow, beige, light brown

The elements and their colours

As our destiny is composed of these five basic elements, the dominating elements in our destiny impact on our taste. For example, if someone has plenty of water in her destiny, she may favour black and gray for her dresses. This does not mean that her favourable colour is black. It only shows that the dominating influence in her destiny is water.

Similarly with designers – if a designer has many fire elements in his destiny, he may tend to use red as the theme of his designs. Let us look at the following example:

HOUR	DAY	MONTH	YEAR
?	庚 Metal	己 Earth	丙 Fire
?	戊 Earth	亥 Water	戊 Earth

52	42	32	22	12	2
乙 Wood	甲 Wood	癸 Water	壬 Water	辛 Metal	庚 Metal
巳 Fire	辰 Earth	卯 Wood	寅 Wood	丑 Earth	子 Water

The Pillars of Destiny of Mr Gianni Versace

The above destiny belongs to famous Italian fashion designer Gianni Versace. Mr Versace was born on a day of metal on earth. Although born in winter with water exhausting the metal, he has a number of earth elements to support his metal. His metal can thus be considered strong and dominant. If metal is the dominating influence in his destiny, this influence should be strongly reflected in his designs and we should expect to see much gold, silver, yellow and metallic colours in his designs. And indeed he is renowned for his Renaissance designs featuring elegant golden and silvery colours.

Some designers use a mixture of colours, making it difficult to distinguish what elements dominate their destiny without examining their birth data. However, many adopt a colour theme that makes their work more easily distinguishable. From examining these main colour themes, I can then try to guess which elements dominate the destinies of these top designers. The following are some of my guesses:

Gianni Versace —	Metal
Jean Paul Gaultier —	Wood
Giorgio Armani —	Earth and Wood
Donna Karen —	Water and Wood
Moschino —	Metal and Fire
Chanel —	Water and Metal
Prada —	Water

Famous designers and their likely elements

In general, most ladies would unconsciously choose the colour of their dominating elements in their destiny. Ladies of strong metal, for example, may prefer Gianni Versace to Donna Karen. However, from a metaphysical point of view, this way of choosing colours and designers is not effective. That's because the dominating colour in our destiny is usually not our favourable element and so will not enhance our wellbeing.

Let us look at the following destiny which belongs to an air hostess:

HOUR	DAY	MONTH	YEAR
丙 Fire	甲 Wood	丙 Fire	壬 Water
寅 Wood	戌 Earth	午 Fire	子 Water

The Pillars of Destiny of an air hostess

75

She is a wood lady born in the summer season when fire is most prosperous. Her wood is weak and fire is the dominating element in her destiny. However, the weak wood needs support from water, and water, in turn, needs support from metal. Therefore her favourable elements are water, wood and metal. Fire and earth are unfavourable as they exhaust her weak wood energy.

Thanks to the strong fire influence, this lady naturally has many red dresses in her wardrobe! However, as fire is her unfavourable element, dressing in red is not helpful to her destiny. Her favourable elements are water, wood and metal so she should wear more black and white and perhaps designer brands like Chanel, Donna Karen and Prada.

The Right Accessories

The same method can be applied when choosing accessories. We should choose accessories according to our favourable element. In the field of accessories, there is both choice of colour and material. Silver and gold jewellery usually belong to the metal element. Most stones, including jade and diamond, belong to the earth category, except red-coloured stones which belong to the fire element, and black-coloured stones which belong to the water element. The most beneficial accessories for our air hostess example are gold, silver, black stones and green jade.

Beauty and Skin Care

When we talk about fashion and accessories, we should also consider beauty and skin care as this is very much related to health. The basic idea is to achieve a balance of elements in our body (readers can refer to earlier chapters for a more thorough discussion on how the five basic elements affect our health). The following are some tips for beauty and skin care.

Figure – As most ladies are very concerned about their figure, let us examine how the principle of the five elements can be applied to control our weight. In Chinese metaphysics, the earth element symbolises the stomach, flesh and body cells. The stronger the earth element in our destiny, the stronger our digestive system. With more earth we can build stronger muscles and gain a better figure. On the other hand, too much earth can make us fat.

The fire element represents our blood circulation. Fire gives birth to earth, so our muscles will be stronger with the support of better blood circulation. The general rule is that we will gain weight with excessive amounts of fire and earth. Metal and water, on the other hand, will help us lose weight as they can exhaust fire and earth. Weight watchers should therefore check whether the fire and earth elements are excessively strong in their destiny. If this is the case, they should eat more fresh fruit and vegetables and less meat, and exercise more during a year of fire and earth.

Hair – In Chinese medicine, hair is symbolised by the wood element. So the stronger the wood in our destiny, the healthier our hair. Wood, like all plants, needs water and the warmth of the sun. So water and fire are essential to keep our hair healthy. People with wood but little water in their destiny may become bald as the wood (or the hair) dries up without enough water. If fire is lacking, the wood may become too cold, causing gray or white hair. Fire refers to blood circulation and water the kidney. If you seem to be losing hair, your kidney could be weak. You may need to eat more fresh fruit and vegetables to enhance the kidney. If you notice your hair turning gray, check your blood circulation and take food supplements that can enhance your blood. Your hair will be healthier with a good balance of water and fire.

Skin care – The metal element is mainly responsible for our skin and breathing system. Ladies with beautiful skin often have a balanced amount of metal in their destiny. Too strong a fire destroys metal, causing dry skin or wrinkles. For healthy skin, avoid taking too much food associated with the fire element. Such food includes deep fried food and food with chilli. On the other hand, too much water can exhaust the metal element and leave the skin looking pale and unhealthy. When this happens take food supplements that can enhance the blood to improve the condition of the skin

The Death of Versace

Just at the time of writing this chapter, the world was shocked by the brutal murder of Mr Gianni Versace on 15 July 1997. He was shot dead at the entrance of his home at Miami Beach, Florida. Let us briefly re-examine his four pillars to see how this abrupt termination of a brilliant life is reflected in his destiny.

I am an ardent fan of Mr Versace and often wear Versace ties. But at the start of 1997, I began to switch to JPG ties. When my friends noticed this, they asked me why. My reply was that Mr Jean Paul Gaultier was in better luck in 1997 as his destiny is dominated by wood and 1997, being a year of strong earth, means money to him. On the other hand Mr Versace is dominated by metal and the earth of 1997 makes the metal excessive. So he is not in good luck.

When I made this remark, I had not obtained Mr Versace's birth data so my belief that he is a metal person was based only on my observation that he uses much gold and silver in his designs. My deduction was proved correct when his birth date was published in the newspapers after his murder. The three known pillars of Mr Versace show that he is a metal person surrounded by many earth elements. As earth supports metal, earth is his resource that gives him the talent and knowledge to create beautiful designs. Being a strong metal person, he needs water and wood, his symbols of creativity and money. His unfavourable elements are earth, which suppresses his water talents, and fire, which generates stronger earth. Using this hypothesis, we can see that he enjoyed good luck with great success during the luck pillars from age 22 to 42. The strong wood and water elements enabled him to express his talents in the fashion industry, which is symbolised by wood. Wood, of course, symbolises the considerable amounts of money he made. After the age of 42, he entered a new luck pillar of wood over earth. The wood element, governing the period from age 42 to 47, still generated much money for him. These successes were also supported by the strong water years from 1992 to 1996. And so, as his designs gained greater popularity, he continued to ruled the fashion world. 1997, however, was a year of fire and earth, both unfavourable elements. Mr Versace, at the age of 50, entered the second half of his luck pillar which is dominated by earth. He was thus into a year of bad luck in 1997.

Mr Versace was murdered on 15 July 1997 at about 7.00 a.m. This date can be expressed as follows in the Four Pillars:

HOUR	DAY	MONTH	YEAR
丙 Fire	戊 Earth	丁 Fire	丁 Fire
辰 Earth	午 Fire	未 Earth	丑 Earth

The date of the murder: 15 July 1997, 7.00 a.m.

The date bears no other elements except fire and earth. The strong fire in the heavenly stems furiously attacked Mr Versace's metal, totally annihilating his single metal element.

Mr Versace's killer was found dead about a week after the murder. The man, Mr Andrew Cunanan, was born on 31 August 1969. His destiny reveals him to be an earth man. Interestingly, the date of the murder, 15 July 1997, is also an earth day. To an earth person, earth symbolises colleagues. The earth element appearing on that day symbolises that he would meet a person and the elements surrounding that earth day reflect what will happen to the person he meets. If we examine the Four Pillars of the day of the murder again, we can see that the earth is in serious trouble as it is too strong. It is suffocated by the overwhelming fire. This symbolises that the person he meets on that day, represented by earth, will die, whether by his hand or in his presence …

Farewell Lady Diana

1997 was perhaps one of the most unfortunate years ever for celebrities. When the world was still grieving over the tragic death of fashion designer Mr Gianni Versace, another tragic event on 31 August 1997 sent even greater shock waves round the world. That day Lady Diana died in a car crash in a Paris tunnel while trying to escape from the paparazzi.

Lady Diana was the most watched woman in the world and her life has been full of drama. In one of my previous books *Feng Shui: The Pillars of Destiny* I have commented on her married life and examined her compatibility with Prince Charles. In the chapter entitled 'The Married Life of Charles and Diana', I remarked that 'Princess Diana is now in an unfavourable luck pillar of earth ...' The book was published in 1994. The unfortunate luck pillar I referred to is the period in Lady Diana's life after the age of 32, which is a luck pillar of strong earth on earth.

Lady Diana's Pillars

Let us examine her Four Pillars of Destiny again. Lady Diana was born on 1 July 1961. At the time I wrote *Feng Shui: The Pillars of Destiny*, her birth hour was not known to me. I later discovered a wonderful book by respected astrologer Ms Rodden. This book provides a treasure trove of birth data of many celebrities, including Lady Diana. In this book, two possible birth hours are given. One is around 7.45 p.m., another around 2.00 p.m. I believe that the latter is more likely as it matches the events that took place. The following is the full set of Four Pillars of Destiny for Lady Diana, taking 2.00 p.m. as her birth hour:

HOUR	DAY	MONTH	YEAR
癸 Water	乙 Wood	甲 Wood	辛 Metal
未 Earth	未 Earth	午 Fire	丑 Earth

42	32	22	12	2
己 Earth	戊 Earth	丁 Fire	丙 Fire	乙 Wood
亥 Water	戊 Earth	酉 Metal	申 Metal	未 Earth

The Pillars of Destiny of Lady Diana (1/7/61)

Lady Diana was born on a day of wood. She is thus a wood lady. This wood is quite weak as it is surrounded by many earth elements, which exhaust her wood energy. She needs more support from water and wood, her most favourable elements. Metal can generate stronger water so it is also helpful and can be regarded as her second best element. On the other hand, earth and fire which exhaust her wood energy are her unfavourable elements.

If we examine her Four Pillars more closely, we can observe that her wood is merely supported by the water element in her hour pillar, and this water, in turn, is supported by the metal element in the year pillar. Without this metal, the water cannot survive and neither can the two wood elements. The metal element in her year pillar is thus of paramount importance.

To a wood lady, metal is the element that conquers her self. So metal is the symbol of her husband, or male lover in her life, and will bring her good luck by generating stronger water, her needed resource element. Her luck pillars show that she encountered very strong metal elements in her second and third luck pillars. These strong metal influences prevailed from around the age of 17 until the age of 32. Metal symbolises her husband and it was during this period that Princess Diana was married to Prince Charles, a very strong husband in terms of status. This was also a period of good fortune as metal is her second best element, generating her needed water resources.

If water is your favourable element, the best way to encounter it is in your luck pillars. But if you are not so fortunate, encountering your second best element supporting the most favourable water is still a good remedy. There are also other means of getting your needed element. The easiest way is to place yourself in an environment with your most favourable element. In Lady Diana's case, she could live near water or the beach. She could even wear more black or grey or decorate her home with these colours. But the most effective external means to get your needed element is to marry a person who has plenty of your favourable elements in his destiny. For Lady Diana, a husband of strong water is very suitable. And water is exactly the element strongly present in Prince Charles' destiny.

Prince Charles

The following is Prince Charles' Four Pillars of Destiny:

HOUR	DAY	MONTH	YEAR
癸 Water	癸 Water	癸 Water	戊 Earth
亥 Water	卯 Wood	亥 Water	子 Water

The Pillars of Destiny of Prince Charles

Prince Charles was born in a year of water, a month of water, a day of water and an hour of water. He is eminently capable of providing Lady Diana with the water she needs. Even though the marriage turned sour later on, I cannot help but opine that Prince Charles is still a compatible partner for Lady Diana.

(Readers can refer to *Feng Shui: The Pillars of Destiny* for a detailed analysis of their compatibility.)

As Lady Diana entered her new luck pillar at the age of 32, she left behind her good metal element and came under the unfavourable influence of earth. The act of leaving behind her good metal can be interpreted as separation from her husband. This was exactly what happened in 1993, when Lady Diana turned 32.

Although Lady Diana was under the bad luck of the unfavourable earth from 1993, no significant misfortune befell her between 1993 and 1996. The reason is that these years before 1997 were mostly water years. The water element from the year pillars gave her the nourishment and resources she needed. However, entering the ten-year earth luck pillar was like stepping onto a mine field. The danger was ever present and it would only take a year of strong earth to trigger a tragedy.

1997, a year of fire and earth, was exactly that dangerous year. The tragedy eventually occurred on 31 August 1997. The following are the Four Pillars of the moment when the accident happened:

HOUR	DAY	MONTH	YEAR
丙	乙	戊	丁
Fire	Wood	Earth	Fire
子	巳	申	丑
Water	Fire	Metal	Earth

The time of the accident: around 0035 hours on 31/8/97

This is a month of strong earth in the heavenly stem. This strong earth, together with the strong earth in Lady Diana's luck pillar, annihilated the water element in her hour pillar. But there is still a ray of hope – the metal element in Lady Diana's year pillar. If this metal survives, it may be able to save the water and thus save Lady Diana's weak wood. Unfortunately, even this metal was in danger as the day was a day of yin wood, which clashed with the yin metal. To compound matters, the accident occurred during an hour of yang fire in the heavenly stem. The yang fire combined with the yin metal, snatching away the yin metal from Lady Diana's destiny. Once the metal in her year pillar was extinguished, the water element in her hour pillar was crushed by the overwhelming earth. With the support of water gone, Lady Diana's wood fell like a domino.

The combination of elements on that day also reflect the scene of the accident. There were three wood elements present: one in Lady Diana's day pillar, one in her month pillar, and one on the day of accident. As Lady Diana is a wood lady, the other two wood elements symbolise two other persons who accompanied her – the driver and the bodyguard. What about the fourth man – Mr Dodi Al Fayed? He is a very close friend or even would-be husband so he is symbolised not by wood, but by the metal present in Lady Diana's year pillar. When this metal crashed against the wood of that day, the metal collapsed, symbolising the instant death of Mr Al Fayed. Metal also represents our lungs so the demise of the metal signified the serious injury Lady Diana's lungs suffered.

When the accident happened, Lady Diana was besieged by heavy earth elements. The tunnel, the pillars, the walls – these are all earth elements. Could she have avoided such tragedy? Would she have been saved if she had stayed on with Prince Charles, who would have provided her with the water element she needed? Fate remains a deep mystery and unfortunately we do not have a time machine with which to travel back …

The Monica Lewinsky Affair

Earlier, we have examined romance, marriage and relationships. Such a discussion would not be complete without a look at perhaps the world's most famous couple, President Bill Clinton and First Lady Hillary Clinton, and the controversial love affair between President Clinton and Ms Monica Lewinsky which was revealed to the public in full details in the Starr Report in September 1998.

It would be a good exercise to study the Four Pillars of Destiny of these three people and examine how the affair is revealed in their respective birth data.

The following are the Four Pillars of President Clinton:

HOUR	DAY	MONTH	YEAR
庚 Metal	乙 Wood	丙 Fire	丙 Fire
辰 Earth	丑 Earth	申 Metal	戌 Earth

67	57	47	37	27	17	7
癸 Water	壬 Water	辛 Metal	庚 Metal	己 Earth	戊 Earth	丁 Fire
卯 Wood	寅 Wood	丑 Earth	子 Water	亥 Water	戌 Earth	酉 Metal

The Pillars of Destiny of President Bill Clinton

President Clinton is a gentleman of yin wood born in the autumn season. This wood is surrounded by very strong metal elements, the most prosperous element in autumn. To a wood gentleman, the metal element represents his power and status. President Clinton's Four Pillars thus reflect he is a very powerful man, commensurate with his position as President of the United States. In an earlier chapter Finding the Right Partner, we have already examined President Clinton's destiny in detail. We had concluded that as his wood element is extremely weak, his destiny falls into a special category called 'Follow the Leader'. The implication is that any element that supports his leader – metal – will bring him good luck, and any element that supports him – wood – will be unfavourable.

This hypothesis has been proved correct as President Clinton is in deep trouble in 1998, a year of strong wood (Tiger). This wood is also in clash with his metal (Monkey) in his month pillar. Wood is a symbol of friends or enemies. In 1998, he faces serious challenges from enemies attempting to demolish his power – metal.

What the Flowers of Romance Reveal ...

Many accusations have been hurled against the President but all of them arise from his affair with White House intern Ms Monica Lewinsky. Can the Four Pillars of the President reveal his conduct towards women? As seen in a previous chapter, we can use a tool called the 'Flowers of Romance'. If we examine the President's Four Pillars, the Flowers of Romance do not appear. There is no Rat, Rooster, Rabbit or Horse in his Four Pillars or luck pillars. He is thus not a particularly flirtatious man. Metal is power and discipline. The strong metal in his destiny shows that he possesses considerable self-restraint.

However, he possesses three earth elements in his earthly branches. Earth is the element conquered by wood and symbolises women to a wood gentleman. There is also an earth element present in his current luck pillar. With four earth elements, it is not surprising then that he has plenty of opportunities to encounter lady admirers and develop some relationships. All these earth elements are in the earthly branches, meaning they are private and hidden. They are however exposed in 1998 and 1999 as both these years have earth elements in the heavenly stems. 1998 is yang earth on wood while 1999 is yin earth on wood. Let us now see how such a crisis is revealed in the First Lady's Four Pillars of Destiny:

HOUR	DAY	MONTH	YEAR
丙 Fire	戊 Earth	庚 Metal	丁 Fire
辰 Earth	寅 Wood	戌 Earth	亥 Water

64	54	44	34	24	14	4
丁 Fire	丙 Fire	乙 Wood	甲 Wood	癸 Water	壬 Water	辛 Metal
巳 Fire	辰 Earth	卯 Wood	寅 Wood	丑 Earth	子 Water	亥 Water

The Pillars of Destiny of Mrs Hillary Clinton

Mrs Clinton is a lady of earth. This earth element is quite strong as it has the support of other earth elements on the earthly branches and fire elements on the heavenly stems. Her day pillar is earth standing on wood. As wood is the element that conquers earth, this wood symbolises her husband – President Clinton. The First Lady's luck pillars show that she has been under the influence of very strong wood since the age of 34. This wood obviously strengthens her husband's position. The powerful wood element also reflects the political achievements of President Clinton in the past 15 years. In 1998, at the age of 51, the First Lady is still in a luck pillar of strong wood, meaning that her husband is still going strong. This luck pillar will last until she is 54.

The wood symbolising the President in the First Lady's destiny is surrounded by earth elements on both sides. As Mrs Clinton is an earth lady, the other earth elements symbolise other ladies. It is therefore not surprising that many other women are attracted to her husband. In 1998 earth appears on the year heavenly stem, symbolising the coming out into the open of such a woman who was previously hidden in the earthly branches.

If we apply the technique of the 'Flowers of Romance', we see that her House of Spouse – the President – is symbolised by the Tiger. The Flower of Romance for the Tiger is the Rabbit, and this Rabbit appears in her current luck pillar between 44 and 54 years. This shows that her husband is under the influence of the Flowers of Romance.

Finally, let us examine the Four Pillars of Ms Monica Lewinsky:

HOUR	DAY	MONTH	YEAR
壬 Water	庚 Metal	己 Earth	癸 Water
午 Fire	申 Metal	未 Earth	丑 Earth

65	55	45	35	25	15	5
丙 Fire	乙 Wood	甲 Wood	癸 Water	壬 Water	辛 Metal	庚 Metal
寅 Wood	丑 Earth	子 Water	亥 Water	戌 Earth	酉 Metal	申 Metal

The Pillars of Destiny of Ms Monica Lewinsky

Ms Lewinsky is a metal lady. Her metal is strong as it is supported by earth. To examine her romance aspects, we need to look at the fire in her hour pillar. As fire conquers metal, the fire element symbolises her male partners or husband. This fire is a Horse. Ms Lewinsky's birth year is the Ox, which takes the Horse as its Flower of Romance. Thus the fire element in her hour pillar not only represents man, but also symbolises romance in her life. If we look deeper into Ms Lewinsky's romance aspects, we see that the fire element is unfortunately quite weak as there is no wood to support it. Moreover the luck pillars that she has gone through in the past are all metal, which have exhausted the strength of the fire. The weakness of the fire element suggests that it will not be easy for her to find a suitable man and develop a lasting relationship. The man she encounters will be just a Flower of Romance. In an earlier chapter, we explained that this means there is 'yuen' but no 'fan' in such a relationship – there is attraction but this attraction cannot develop into a serious and permanent relationship. Such a man appeared when the fire element was stimulated – in 1995 (a year of wood stimulating the fire), 1996 (a year of fire standing on water) and 1997 (a year of fire standing on earth).

President Clinton and Ms Lewinsky are attracted to each other. The President's favourable element is metal and Ms Lewinsky is a strong metal lady. The day pillars of the President and Ms Lewinsky also enjoy a combine relationship. The President is yin wood while Ms Lewinsky is yang metal. These two will thus be strongly attracted to each other and combine. As Ms Lewinsky testified in Mr Kenneth Starr's investigation, "there had been a chemistry that was there before and we were both attracted to each other ..." Metal conquers wood, so Ms Lewinsky (being yang metal) takes more initiative in the affair.

The fire in Ms Lewinsky's destiny is however weak and vulnerable to attack. In 1998, Ms Lewinsky had just turned 25 and entered a luck pillar of water. This water attacked her fire, symbolising that her man was in trouble.

The purpose of this analysis is to present an exercise on the application of the techniques we have discussed in the previous chapters of this book. The points made are solely logical deductions from the facts as revealed by the five elements in our destiny.

CHILDREN

Children in Our Destiny

Besides marriage, an important part of metaphysical consulting is the giving of advice on children. A feng shui consultant is frequently asked by young wives how many children they will have.

Unfortunately, this question has become increasingly difficult to answer. The technique of the Four Pillars of Destiny can help reveal the number of children one can have, but with modern contraceptives, this number can be controlled by you. Even if your Four Pillars of Destiny show that you can have 10 children, you can exercise restraint and cut that number down to one or two. So while it is possible to predict the number of chances to give birth, it is not possible to tell how many children you will actually have. For example, we may see as many as five chances in the destiny of a Chinese woman, but in China, where strict birth control is exercised, the lady may only give birth to one child.

Despite this drawback, the Four Pillars of Destiny still allow us to view our relationship with our children and foresee events affecting them. Just as we have identified the earthly branch of our day pillar as our House of Spouse, we can also identify the hour pillar as the house of our children. In general, the heavenly stem of the day pillar represents our son and the earthly branch of our day pillar represents our daughter. If we have only sons or daughters, then the entire hour pillar represents our children.

Mia Farrow

To examine our relationship with our children, we only need to compare our self element and the element of our House of Spouse with the hour pillar. Returning to the example of Ms Mia Farrow, her hour pillar is metal over fire and her day pillar is earth over metal. Looking at the heavenly stems, her earth self gives birth to and supports the metal of her hour pillar – this shows that Ms Farrow is a very supportive mother. As for the earthly branches, the fire in the hour pillar destroys the metal of the day pillar. This suggests that the children – represented by the hour pillar – are not afraid of their father, who is symbolised by the House of Spouse in Ms Farrow's destiny. Fire is favourable to Ms Farrow so the presence of strong fire in the earthly branch of the hour pillar is a sign that her children will bring her good luck and treat her well.

Like the aspects of husband and wife, the aspects of children are also represented by the elements. For the mother, the child is the element that she gives birth to. If the self is earth, as in the example of Ms Farrow, the children are symbolised by metal, the offspring of earth. For a man, his children are the offspring of his wife. For example, if the father is a metal man, the mother is symbolised by the element conquered by metal – wood. Wood gives birth to fire so the metal man's children are represented by the fire element. Another way of looking at this is to think of the children element in a man's destiny as the element that destroys the self, similar to the power and status element.

Lin Ching Hsia

Let us look at the example of Ms Lin Ching Hsia again. Previously we discussed her happy marriage to a fashion tycoon. She later gave birth to a daughter in 1995.

HOUR	DAY	MONTH	YEAR
辛 Metal	癸 Water	甲 Wood	甲 Wood
酉 Metal	亥 Water	戌 Earth	午 Fire

The Pillars of Destiny of Ms Lin Ching Hsia

Ms Lin is a lady of water. The offspring of water is wood and, appropriately enough, she gave birth to her first child in 1995 – a year of strong wood.

As explained earlier, the month pillar represents the parents, the day pillar the self and the spouse, and the hour pillar the children. This is a handy way to examine the relationship between the self and the children. The best configuration is when the hour pillar contains the elements most favourable to the self.

Take the example of a man with weak fire who needs the support of wood. If he was born in the hour of wood, his children will be supportive and will bring him good fortune. In this case, I would usually recommend that he has children as early as possible. If wood also appears on the heavenly stem of his hour pillar, it implies that the child will have a harmonious relationship with him. On the other hand, if this fire person's hour pillar has a heavenly stem of water, the child will dominate him or be difficult to control because water destroys fire.

This example illustrates how we can list out a person's Four Pillars and predict his likely relationship with his children.

Let us now return to Ms Farrow's destiny:

HOUR	DAY	MONTH	YEAR
庚 Metal	己 Earth	戊 Earth	乙 Wood
午 Fire	酉 Metal	寅 Wood	酉 Metal

The Pillars of Destiny of Ms Mia Farrow

Ms Farrow is an earth lady. Her favourable element is fire which provides support and resources for her weak earth. Her hour pillar is metal over fire. As the earth self gives birth to metal, this shows that Ms Farrow is very fond and supportive of her children. The fire earthly branch of her hour pillar is her favourable element, indicating that her children will reciprocate their mother's support. However, the earthly branch of the day pillar – representing the House of Spouse to Mia – is metal, which is threatened by the fire in the earthly branch of the hour pillar, symbolising her children. This implies that despite the children's harmonious relationship with Ms Farrow, they may not get along with the father.

In the case of Ms Lin Ching Hsia, she is a weak water lady who needs the support of metal. There are strong metal elements in her hour pillar, symbolising that her children will be supportive of her. Ms Lin's day pillar is water over water and her hour pillar metal over metal. The metal hour pillar, therefore, not only supports her self, but also her House of Spouse. This paints a picture of a harmonious family with the children loving both parents.

Choosing a Good Birthday

In Hong Kong it has becoming increasingly popular for mothers to choose birth by Caesarean operation over natural birth. If a couple decides against natural birth, they will often consult a feng shui expert to select an auspicious birth date for their baby. As the Four Pillars of Destiny are derived from a person's birth data and reveal much of his future fortune, it is important to plan carefully.

How Reliable is 'Artificial' Birth Data?

There is, however, controversy over whether a set of 'chosen' birth data really reflects the destiny of the child. Some believe such birth data does not follow natural laws, making the accuracy of this man-made destiny doubtful. These sceptics appear to have a point. As we have seen, our individual destiny is not totally independent. Each of us comes from a family with parents, brothers and sisters. A set of Four Pillars of Destiny reveals not only the fortunes of that single person, but also that of his parents and siblings. The month pillar represents a person's parents as well as their fortune in relation to the self. If we select a date to give birth to a child arbitrarily or at random, the month pillar of this man-made destiny may not match the child's family background or the fortunes of his parents. For example, a child born to a carpenter ought to possess a month pillar showing that his father is a carpenter. If a carpenter's wife arbitrarily chooses the birthday of a prince to give birth, paradox and confusion will arise. The boy will possess a set of pillars belonging to a prince even though he is only the son of a carpenter. The month pillar of these artificial pillars will not reflect the true family background of the boy. Thus one school of thought dismisses 'artificial' birth data as unreliable for destiny analysis.

During my years of practice, I have examined the Four Pillars of Destiny of a number of children born by Caesarean section and have, to my surprise, found that their artificial destiny can still be analysed in the usual way, with a degree of accuracy no less than that of those born naturally. Let me offer my opinion here. Scientists and philosophers are forever debating the subject of free will versus destiny. But does free will exist at all? We live in a Universe governed by the laws of nature, such as the physical laws of motion, gravity, thermodynamics and so on. All our actions are governed by such laws. It appears then that our free will to make choices and decisions is an illusion. Are we really making decisions independent of the laws of nature, or are such decisions in fact subject to the laws of nature, or even planted into our heads in accordance with the laws of nature?

This seems to be an eternal mystery of life. The system of the Four Pillars of Destiny postulates that the interrelationships of the five basic elements shown in the Chinese calendar (and hence in our birth data) are reflections of the laws of nature. As every matter and every event in this world is governed by this natural order of the five elements, it follows that all the choices and decisions we make are also subject to such order. Selecting an artificial birth data for a child is also a choice that must comply with natural laws. Theoretically, therefore, we do not have the freedom to select a set of birth data that opposes the laws of the five elements. So selecting the birthday of a prince for a baby born to a carpenter is impossible because this is against the laws of the elements.

My past experience with artificial birth data suggests that selecting a set of birth data which does not match the family background will never work out. If such a mismatched date is chosen, something will usually arise to prevent the operation from being carried out at the chosen time. For example, there may be no mismatching dates within the range given by the doctor or the baby may come out earlier than expected or the doctor may not be available at the chosen time to perform the operation and so on. If an artificially mismatched birthday can never happen, it follows that only those who choose to give birth on a date that matches the background of the baby will succeed. Such birth data, though artificial, still reflects the destiny of the baby, simply because it follows the laws of the five elements and hence the laws of nature.

I have applied the technique of the Four Pillars of Destiny to artificially chosen Caesarean birth data for quite a number of babies. Thus far I have found that their destiny can be analysed in the usual way. Nevertheless, my pool of samples is limited and most are still babies at the time of writing. I will need to collect more examples and look further into the future of these babies to verify my opinion.

As a person's birth data is like a cosmic code showing his destiny and future development, the person choosing this birth data holds great responsibility in his hands. This is a very important task that must be handled with utmost care. The Four Pillars of the newborn baby not only affect the baby's future, but also reflect the fortunes of his parents. So besides selecting a good future for the baby, it is important to ensure that the baby's pillars show reasonably good fortune for the parents at least during his growing up years before he becomes independent. The mother's safety when giving birth must also be considered, so the birth date should be auspicious for her too.

In addition, the child's Four Pillars should preferably be compatible with those of his parents. For example, if the parents' favourable element is metal, it is best to select a birthday with plenty of metal to help create harmony within the family. Avoid clashes or conflict between the day and month pillars of the baby's destiny, as discord in this area reflects disharmony with the parents. Finding a suitable date that satisfies all these conditions will not be easy, especially since this date has to be chosen from within the limited period the baby is expected to be born. However, most of the pillars, including the year pillar, the month pillar and the luck pillars which are derived from the month pillar, will usually be predetermined. There is often only flexibility to select an appropriate day and hour to match the given year, month and luck pillars.

Chosen Destiny: A Case Study

Let me explain the complexity of this task with a real-life example.

HOUR	DAY	MONTH	YEAR
庚 Metal	乙 Wood	庚 Metal	癸 Water
辰 Earth	未 Earth	申 Metal	卯 Wood

66	56	46	36	26	16	6
丁 Fire	丙 Fire	乙 Wood	甲 Wood	癸 Water	壬 Water	辛 Metal
卯 Wood	寅 Wood	丑 Earth	子 Water	亥 Water	戌 Earth	酉 Metal

The Pillars of Destiny of the mother

97

HOUR	DAY	MONTH	YEAR
己 Earth	甲 Wood	丙 Fire	癸 Water
巳 Fire	辰 Earth	辰 Earth	卯 Wood

68	58	48	38	28	18	8
己 Earth	庚 Metal	辛 Metal	壬 Water	癸 Water	甲 Wood	乙 Wood
酉 Metal	戌 Earth	亥 Water	子 Water	丑 Earth	寅 Wood	卯 Wood

The Pillars of Destiny of the father

My clients are a reasonably affluent couple. The father is from a wealthy and well-known family while the mother is a celebrity in Hong Kong, a former Miss Hong Kong beauty queen. The father is a strong wood person whose favourable elements are fire, earth and metal which provide an outlet for his excessive energy. The mother is a weak wood lady who needs the support of more water and wood. I chose the following set of birth data for her to give Caesarean birth to a baby boy in 1997:

HOUR	DAY	MONTH	YEAR
甲 Wood	丁 Fire	壬 Water	丁 Fire
辰 Earth	酉 Metal	寅 Wood	丑 Earth

67	57	47	37	27	17	7
乙 Wood	丙 Fire	丁 Fire	戊 Earth	己 Earth	庚 Metal	辛 Metal
未 Earth	申 Metal	酉 Metal	戌 Earth	亥 Water	子 Water	丑 Earth

The chosen birthday for the baby boy

The boy was born on 24 February 1997 at about 8.30 a.m. The chosen Four Pillars show that he is a fire boy born in spring with strong support from the prosperous wood in the month pillar. Wood is the mother of fire. To ensure that the mother maintains reasonably strong influence over the child, stronger wood is needed in the configuration. I decided to choose an hour of wood which not only enhances the strength of the mother, but also strengthens the fire boy. Wood also means education, knowledge and resources to a fire boy – good qualities which should be enhanced. Moreover, as wood is also favourable to the mother, a configuration of strong wood in the date of birth helps ensure that the mother has a smooth Caesarean operation.

With the strong support of wood, the baby is now a strong fire boy. His favourable elements are earth and metal which exhaust his excessive fire energy. Water is also favourable as it helps suppress the excessive fire and exert discipline on the boy. His unfavourable elements are wood and fire which are already excessive in his configuration.

The boy's luck pillars, from age 7 to 77, are mostly under the influence of earth, metal and water – his favourable elements. This helps ensure that he has a smooth and successful life, bringing not only good luck to himself but also securing good fortune for his parents during his early years.

Let us examine more closely the destiny I have chosen for the boy. He is a fire person with fire, water and wood in the heavenly stems. Fire represents his colleagues and friends, water his power, status and discipline, and wood his resources and education. As the heavenly stems show a person's outlook, these elements project the image of man with status and resources. However, this does not mean he has no money or skill. The intelligence element of earth is found in the earthly branches of both the year and hour pillars, signifying that the boy is skilful and intelligent. Wood found in the earthly branch of the month pillar indicates a strong foundation of resources, education and knowledge. The metal

99

element, representing his money, is found in the earthly branch of the day pillar, supported by the earth in the hour pillar.

We thus have an intelligent and knowledgeable boy. He is neither rebellious nor overly aggressive as the earth elements lie underneath in the earthly branches. He has money but will not show off as it is also hidden underneath in the day pillar. He is also compatible in personality with his parents as he possesses strong wood elements favourable to his mother, as well as strong fire elements favourable to his father.

The birth data also shows good fortune for his parents, represented by the month pillar. In this example, the month pillar is water over wood. Water in the heavenly stem symbolises the father and wood in the earthly branch represents the mother. Let us look at the father aspect. The water in the heavenly stem of the month pillar is the destroyer of fire. Hence the father exerts control and discipline over the fire baby. However, this domination is not excessive as the son is a strong fire boy who welcomes some control by water. Moreover, it is yang water controlling yin fire. As yang and yin are harmonious, this is a good relationship.

The water symbolising the father stands on a wood earthly branch. Wood is the creative and intelligence element of water and can also produce fire, a symbol of money to the father – a water man. The Four Pillars therefore reflect that the father is an intelligent and skilful businessman. This describes the father, a successful entrepreneur, well. The month pillar shows the water heavenly stem giving birth to the wood earthly branch, symbolising the harmonious relationship between the father and the mother.

Let us now examine the father's fortune as reflected in the child's luck pillars. The father, symbolised by water born in spring, is weak because the water is being exhausted by strong wood and fire. His favourable elements are metal and water, and also earth which supports metal. If we look at the child's luck pillars, we see that the child will pass through these favourable elements of metal, earth and water in his first two luck pillars between 7 and 27. So the father will encounter good fortune as the child grows up.

This example shows that a well-chosen birth date must cater to many different aspects, each of which can be vital to the child or his parents. The birth data has to be compatible with the parents' favourable elements, be auspicious for the mother to give birth, and reflect a stable and bright future not only for the child but also for the parents.

But if such a good set of pillars can be chosen by man, does it mean we have the power to create artificial destiny? The answer is no because this good birth data can work out only if it matches the fortune of the parents and the background of the boy, which are essential factors for the success of such a choice. One further thought is that if the child is destined to be born on such a good date, why do we have to choose at all? Perhaps the boy will still be born on the same date if the mother chooses to give birth naturally. The problem, however, is that if Caesarean birth is selected, an agent is needed to convey the date to the mother. In such a case, we are merely conveying a birth data already determined by the laws of nature.

Understanding Health
Through Our Birth Data

A newborn baby brings much happiness to its parents but this joy is often accompanied by anxiety about its health. All parents naturally wish good health for their children so any illness can be cause for great concern. Not all babies are born with perfect health – a newborn carries with him some inborn qualities which include his personality, temperament, physique and certain weaknesses in health, which as scientists have discovered, can be inherited from his parents' genes.

The system of the Four Pillars of Destiny can reveal considerable information about a person's health as well as inherent weaknesses in his body. Chinese traditional medicine shares the same foundation as the system of the Four Pillars of Destiny. Both are based on the principle of yin and yang and the five basic elements. In Chinese medicine, each of our vital internal organs is assigned an element. The heart is symbolised by fire, stomach by earth, lung by metal, kidney by water and liver by wood. The functional relationships between these vital organs also follow the Cycle of Birth and the Cycle of Destruction of the five elements. The basic philosophy is that if the elements in our body are in balance, we will enjoy good health. Too much or too little of any element can bring about illness or discomfort.

For example, the kidney governs all fluids and water in the body which in turn keep the fire of the heart under control. If the kidney is weak, the water will be weak and unable to control the fire. An uncontrolled fire can cause discomfort of the heart or irregular heartbeat. So although the symptoms show up in the heart, the root of the illness is the kidney. Chinese herbal doctors will often prescribe medicine which enhances the kidney's strength. Once the water of the kidney regains its strength, it will be able to control the fire of the heart and the discomfort will cease. It is thus through the Cycle of Birth and Cycle of Destruction of the five basic elements that Chinese doctors are able to trace a sickness to its root and cure the patient.

The following table shows how the various organs in our body are linked to the five elements.

Metal	—	Lung, respiratory organs, skin, intestines, nose, teeth
Wood	—	Limbs, neck, spinal cord, liver, eyebrows, hair
Water	—	Kidneys, bones, sex organs, ears
Fire	—	Heart, blood, brain, nervous system, eyes, lips
Earth	—	Stomach, muscles, digestive organs, cells

The elements and the parts of the body they symbolise

Our Four Pillars show the composition of the five elements in our body. By analysing the weakness and strength of each of the elements in a person's Four Pillars of Destiny, we can gain a deep insight into his state of health. The overabundance or weakness of an element allows us to pinpoint potentially troublesome organs. For example, if the fire element is too strong or too weak in a set of Four Pillars, the person may be more susceptible to sicknesses relating to fire, such as high blood pressure, heart disease or eye problems. By the same token, if the water is too strong or too weak, it may indicate illnesses of the kidney, sex organs, ear or bones.

O. J. Simpson: Childhood Rickets

Let me illustrate with some examples. Earlier in this book we examined the Four Pillars of Mr O. J. Simpson whose murder trial catapulted him to worldwide notoriety. A little known fact about him is that as a child, he suffered from rickets. This is a deformation of the legs, toes or ankles caused by nutritional deficiency. As a two-year-old boy, Mr Simpson had very skinny and bow-shaped legs.

HOUR	DAY	MONTH	YEAR
戊 Earth	己 Earth	丁 Fire	丁 Fire
辰 Earth	丑 Earth	未 Earth	亥 Water

60	50	40	30	20	10	0
庚 Metal	辛 Metal	壬 Water	癸 Water	甲 Wood	乙 Wood	丙 Fire
子 Water	丑 Earth	寅 Wood	卯 Wood	辰 Earth	巳 Fire	午 Fire

The Pillars of Destiny of Mr O. J. Simpson

How is this illness reflected in his Four Pillars? Mr Simpson is a strong earth person who needs water and metal to release his excessive earth energy. Fire is his enemy. There is a water element in the earthly branch of his year pillar which becomes a very important favourable element to him as it is the only outlet for his excessive earth energy. His first luck pillar from age one to ten was a pillar of strong fire which is unfavourable and affected his health. This strong fire clashed with the water in the earthly branch of his year pillar, damaging the water. Water symbolises bones, and water below represents the lower part of his body. This explains his illness with his leg bones.

Stephen Hawking

Another prominent example is famous British scientist Mr Stephen Hawking whose book *A Brief History of Time* has become an all-time bestseller. Mr Hawking is almost totally immobilised by motor neuron disease. Soon after symptoms started appearing when he was 21, he began to lose control of his muscles and he was eventually confined to an electric wheelchair. The following are his Four Pillars of Destiny:

HOUR	DAY	MONTH	YEAR
?	辛 Metal	辛 Metal	辛 Metal
?	酉 Metal	丑 Earth	巳 Fire

61	51	41	31	21	11	1
甲 Wood	乙 Wood	丙 Fire	丁 Fire	戊 Earth	己 Earth	庚 Metal
午 Fire	未 Earth	申 Metal	酉 Metal	戊 Earth	亥 Water	子 Water

The Pillars of Destiny of Mr Stephen Hawking

Mr Hawking is a very strong metal person. His favourable elements are water and wood which help dissipate this metal energy. His enemies are metal and earth which reinforce his metal. During his youth, he had two luck pillars of water. But when he turned 21, he entered a luck pillar of very strong earth. This unfavourable element upset his health. Earth is a symbol of the stomach, muscles and body cells and in his case, the excessive earth brought about serious muscle problems.

Ray Charles: Tragedy in His Destiny

Famous American jazz and soul singer Mr Ray Charles lost his eyesight at the age of six in an accident and his dark glasses became his trademark. Let us see how his Four Pillars reflect this tragedy.

HOUR	DAY	MONTH	YEAR
?	丙 Fire	乙 Wood	庚 Metal
?	子 Water	酉 Metal	午 Fire

65	55	45	35	25	15	5
壬 Water	辛 Metal	庚 Metal	己 Earth	戊 Earth	丁 Fire	丙 Fire
辰 Earth	卯 Wood	寅 Wood	丑 Earth	子 Water	亥 Water	戌 Earth

The Pillars of Destiny of Mr Ray Charles

Mr Ray Charles is a fire person born in autumn when the metal element is most prosperous. The many metal elements in his Four Pillars exhaust the fire energy so his fire is weak and needs support from wood and more fire. He has a wood element in the heavenly stem of his month pillar but this wood is too weak to be of any help as it stands on and sits next to metal, which undermines the wood. The only support his fire can hope for is from the fire element in the earthly branch of his year pillar.

The year 1936, when he was six years old, was a year of fire over water. Fire on water is weak fire because it symbolises the fire being extinguished by water. This was also the year of the Rat. As Mr Charles was born in the year of the Horse, the water of the Rat year clashed with the fire of the Horse in Mr Charles' year pillar and extinguished it. Fire symbolises the blood, the heart, the nervous system and the eyes. In Mr Charles' case, his eyes were tragically blinded.

I can quote many more examples to show how the weakening of a favourable element can cause serious illness relating to that element. Ms Teresa Teng suffered from asthma because of the weakness in the metal in her destiny. This eventually triggered a heart attack and caused her death. Mr Christopher Reeve, well-known for his role as Superman in several popular movies, encountered a metal-wood clash in his destiny. This caused a horseriding accident which left him with a broken back – wood is a symbol of the neck, the backbone and the spinal cord. Tennis champion Monica Seles was stabbed in the back in 1994 because she encountered a similar clash between the metal and the wood in her destiny. Mr Brandon Lee – the son of Mr Bruce Lee – was killed by a bullet which broke his back; again this occurred during a clash between the wood and the metal in his destiny.

The evidence that the elements in our Four Pillars of Destiny are directly linked to our health and wellbeing is overwhelming. So a good understanding of the elements helps us anticipate weaknesses in our body from childhood. With such knowledge, children can be given appropriate food supplements to help remedy weaknesses before they become serious.

Child Tragedies

To bring up a child with good health, good conduct and a good education is not easy. Besides health problems, factors such as carelessness or negligence can lead to injury or even death in a child. However, in many cases, it is possible to foresee such dangers in a child's Four Pillars of Destiny.

Christmas Murder: JonBenet Ramsey

One such tragedy occurred during the 1996 Christmas holidays. Six-year-old JonBenet Ramsey was found dead in the basement of her home in Boulder, Colorado on Boxing Day. She had been strangled and her mother later discovered a ransom note demanding US$118,000. This mysterious case captured nationwide attention and at the time of writing, the unknown killer is still at large.

JonBenet Ramsey was born on 6 August 1990. By the age of six, she was already a beauty pageant veteran who had captured the title of Little Miss Colorado. Let us examine her birth data to see how this tragedy is reflected in her destiny:

HOUR	DAY	MONTH	YEAR
?	癸 Water	癸 Water	庚 Metal
?	卯 Wood	未 Earth	午 Fire

29	19	9
庚 Metal 辰 Earth	辛 Metal 巳 Fire	壬 Water 午 Fire

The Pillars of Destiny of Ms JonBenet Ramsey

Her birth data shows that she is a water girl born in the year of the Horse. Her water is quite weak as she was born in an earth month in summer with strong fire and wood exhausting her water. She needs the support of metal and water. Fire and earth are her enemies who exhaust and destroy her water energy.

In a previous chapter, I briefly introduced the concept of earthly branches clashing. All such clashes involve opposing elements. When one arrives at a year with an animal sign in clash against one's year of birth, it could signal a less harmonious year ahead for the person. If this clash affects important elements in one's Four Pillars of Destiny, it may even cause a tragedy. JonBenet Ramsey was born in the year of the Horse and 1996 was the year of the Rat. Because the Rat is a water element and the Horse a fire element, these signs clash. And as this occurs in the year pillar, this is traditionally called 'offending the Grand Duke of the Year' and often signals serious trouble.

In a set of Four Pillars, as explained previously, the year pillar symbolises the grandparents, the month pillar the parents and so on. However, we can also divide the Four Pillars into different ages – the year pillar symbolises childhood, the month pillar youth, the day pillar middle age, and the hour pillar old age.

In Ms Ramsey's case, the clash at age seven is especially serious. First, fire is her unfavourable element. So any clash between fire and water will stir up the unfavourable effect of the fire element in her year pillar which symbolises her childhood.

Second, December 1996 is near the end of the year of the Rat and 1997 is the year of the Ox – a year of fire over earth, both unfavourable elements to Ms Ramsey. I have noticed many occasions where if the following year is extremely bad, its impact often arrives earlier at the end of the previous year. The advance arrival of the bad year of the Ox brought tragedy to Ms Ramsey.

HOUR	DAY	MONTH	YEAR
?	丙 Fire	庚 Metal	丙 Fire
?	申 Metal	子 Water	子 Water

The date of the murder (26/12/96)

The day of the murder, 26 December 1996, is a day of metal which clashed with Ms Ramsey's wood in her day pillar. So on the day of her death, there was much discord between fire and water as well as metal and wood. Even the fire heavenly stem of the day pillar is in clash against the water of Ms Ramsey's day pillar. When faced with a critical situation, one way to determine whether we can survive the crisis is to look at our future. In Ms Ramsey's case, her immediate future is symbolised by her first luck pillar of water over fire. The earthly branch of fire carries more weight as it is the foundation of the luck pillar. So this luck pillar is unfavourable, with the impact of strong fire. If the future is unfavourable, the chance of survival is slim. Ms Ramsey's death was caused mainly by the various clashes between the elements on 26 December 1996, the most serious being fire against water. Fire was thus the reason behind her tragedy.

Tragedy in New York: Conor Clapton

Another famous child tragedy involved Conor Clapton who fell out from a window left open by a housekeeper on the 53rd floor of his New York City apartment on 20 March 1991. This accident captured worldwide attention because the boy was the son of famous rock guitarist Mr Eric Clapton. The following are the Four Pillars of Conor Clapton:

HOUR	DAY	MONTH	YEAR
癸 Water	丁 Fire	丙 Fire	丙 Fire
卯 Wood	酉 Metal	申 Metal	寅 Wood

25	15	5
己 Earth 亥 Water	戊 Earth 戊 Earth	丁 Fire 酉 Metal

The Pillars of Destiny of Mr Conor Clapton

He is a fire boy born in autumn when metal is most prosperous. The strong metal destroys wood. Wood is the resource to fire, so if wood is weak, the fire will also be weak. Conor Clapton is thus a weak fire boy who needs support from wood and fire. Metal and earth are his unfavourable elements. The earthly branches of his Four Pillars are occupied by two wood and two metal elements and these elements are in clash with each another. The Tiger year is also in conflict with the Monkey month, and the Rooster day in clash with his Rabbit hour. These clashes signify potential danger. Although Conor Clapton has two wood elements supporting his fire in the earthly branches, this wood is weak as he was born in the autumn when wood was being destroyed by metal. In 1991, an unfavourable year of metal and earth, he entered a critical phase in life. On turning five, he entered a luck pillar of fire over metal, with the metal earthly branch dominating. There was thus a very strong metal influence in 1991.

Let us examine the day of the tragedy. The accident took place at around 11 a.m. on 20 March 1991 which can be expressed in the Four Pillars as follows:

HOUR	DAY	MONTH	YEAR
己	己	辛	辛
Earth	Earth	Metal	Metal
巳	丑	卯	未
Fire	Earth	Wood	Earth

The date of the accident (20/3/91)

The moment of the accident is full of metal and earth influences. A wood element is present in the month pillar, but the metal (Rooster) in his first luck pillar clashes directly with the wood (Rabbit) and destroys it. The two wood elements in his earthly branches cannot offer any help as both are being destroyed by metal. With the wood ineffective, he can only hope for help from the two fire elements in the heavenly stems of the year and month pillars. Unfortunately, this pair of yang fire elements cannot help either, as they have combined with the pair of yin metal in the month and year pillars of March 1991.

At this juncture, I need to introduce another aspect of relationships between elements. We have seen that earthly branches can clash with one another. Pairs of earthly branches or heavenly stems can also combine and lose their original properties. Such combine relationships can cause serious trouble if one's favourable element loses its favourable property on combining with another element, or when an unfavourable element is suddenly reinforced when two other elements combine and launches a concerted attack on the self. The following tables show these combine relationships again:

甲 (Yang Wood)	—	己 (Yin Earth)	
丙 (Yang Fire)	—	辛 (Yin Metal)	
戊 (Yang Earth)	—	癸 (Yin Water)	
庚 (Yang Metal)	—	乙 (Yin Wood)	
壬 (Yang Water)	—	丁 (Yin Fire)	

The combine relationships of the heavenly stems

子 (Water) Rat   —   丑 (Earth) Ox

寅 (Wood) Tiger   —   亥 (Water) Pig

卯 (Wood) Rabbit   —   戌 (Earth) Dog

辰 (Earth) Dragon   —   酉 (Metal) Rooster

巳 (Fire) Snake   —   申 (Metal) Monkey

午 (Fire) Horse   —   未 (Earth) Goat

The combine relationships of the earthly branches

But there is also another type of combine relationship, which I would like to introduce now, that creates very powerful elemental influences. These relationships need three earthly branches to form. There are four sets of three-element combination relationships. They are:

申 Monkey + 子 Rat + 辰 Dragon = Water combination

亥 Pig + 卯 Rabbit + 未 Goat = Wood combination

巳 Snake + 酉 Rooster + 丑 Ox = Metal combination

寅 Tiger + 午 Horse + 戌 Dog = Fire combination

Combinations of three earthly branches

On the day of the accident, 20 March 1991, the Snake and the Ox appeared in the earthly branches of the day and hour pillars. These two combined with the Rooster in Conor Clapton's first luck pillar to form a very strong metal ring of power. It was this strong metal that delivered the fatal blow to the boy's wood support and caused his death.

Death caused by metal and earth can be associated with plunging onto the ground from a great height. In the previous chapter we mentioned that metal symbolises skin. The manner of death portrayed by metal and earth is that of skin crashing onto the ground.

Conor's Death in Eric Clapton's Destiny

Any terrible accident which occurs to a beloved child should be reflected in the Four Pillars of the parents. Let us now look at Mr Eric Clapton's Four Pillars of Destiny. Mr Clapton was born on 30 March 1945.

HOUR	DAY	MONTH	YEAR
辛 Metal	戊 Earth	己 Earth	乙 Wood
酉 Metal	戊 Earth	卯 Wood	酉 Metal

68	58	48	38	28	18	8
壬 Water	癸 Water	甲 Wood	乙 Wood	丙 Fire	丁 Fire	戊 Earth
申 Metal	酉 Metal	戊 Earth	亥 Water	子 Water	丑 Earth	寅 Wood

The Pillars of Destiny of Mr Eric Clapton

He is an earth person born in spring with very strong wood and metal elements. Both wood and metal exhaust or destroy the earth, so Mr Clapton is a weak earth person who needs support from more earth and fire. Metal is given birth by earth and reflects his intelligence and skill. Therefore, the many metal elements in Mr Clapton's destiny symbolise his great musical talent.

To examine Mr Clapton's son, two aspects should be examined. First, the element symbolising his son is wood, which is the offspring of his wife element – water. We can also examine his hour pillar which is his House of Children.

Mr Clapton's Four Pillars show conflict between wood and metal, similar to his son's destiny. Mr Clapton, the father, was born in spring. The wood is strong and clashes with his metal hour pillar, threatening his son. The tragedy occurred in 1991, a year of metal. That year, Mr Clapton was 46 years old and in a luck pillar of strong wood, again another clash between wood and metal. As wood represents his son, the strong metal emerging in 1991 showed that this wood (his son) was into a critical year. On the day of the accident, as we have already explained, strong metal emerged to demolish any wood. The destruction of wood symbolised the death of his son. The clash also affected the metal in his hour pillar, shaking his House of Children.

This sad example illustrates that clues about the wellbeing of our children can be found in our Four Pillars of Destiny as well. It is worthwhile to examine the pillars of both children and parents regularly – at least once a year. If bad signs appear in both sets of pillars, the parents should be more vigilant to avoid misfortune to their children in such an adverse year.

Problems and Talent in Children

Watching a child grow up can be a great joy. However, this exciting stage of life is often accompanied by numerous problems. Every week, mothers anxious about their children come to see me. They ask all sorts of questions about their children's health, education and behaviour – what subjects should their son choose, why is their son rebellious and uncommunicative, why is their daughter not as attentive in class as before, and so on. In this chapter I will show you how the Four Pillars of Destiny can help mothers better understand their children's personality and potential and help them improve their relationship with their children.

With family planning, the size of a typical family is shrinking in many countries. In Hong Kong and China, for example, many young families will only have one child. When this happens, parents often end up showering too much attention on the child, thus hampering the child's self-development or even causing disharmony in his relationship with his parents.

A Problem Child?

The following is a typical example.

HOUR	DAY	MONTH	YEAR
戊 Earth	庚 Metal	戊 Earth	戊 Earth
子 Water	戌 Earth	午 Fire	辰 Earth

67	57	47	37	27	17	7
辛 Metal	壬 Water	癸 Water	甲 Wood	乙 Wood	丙 Fire	丁 Fire
亥 Water	子 Water	丑 Earth	寅 Wood	卯 Wood	辰 Earth	巳 Fire

The Pillars of Destiny of a young girl with problem

This is the destiny of a nine-year-old girl. Her mother first consulted me in 1997, complaining that the girl was lazy and appeared uninterested in her studies. She seldom talked to her parents and her attitude towards her father was somewhat hostile.

On analysis, her Four Pillars help explain such behaviour. She is a metal girl. Although born in summer when fire is strong, this fire is powerless to control her metal as it is surrounded by heavy earth elements which exhaust the fire power. The earth elements are resources and support the metal self. Hence the metal has become too strong and she needs outlets to exhaust her metal energy. Her favourable elements are wood and water. Earth, fire and metal are her enemies which make her earth and metal even more excessive.

Too much earth resource elements made her lazy, introverted and overly cautious, with her intelligence element of water heavily suppressed by the earth. A weak intelligence element means she will not take the initiative to express herself and will lack energy. This behaviour became more marked in 1997, a year of fire and earth. She was also into a luck pillar of fire which generated stronger earth and put heavy pressure on her. Her main problem was that the earth, supported by fire, was suppressing and overwhelming the single outlet for her metal energy – the water element in her hour pillar.

How can we help her? The month pillar, which symbolises her parents, is occupied by very strong earth supported by fire. The unfavourable earth element in the month pillar, symbolising the father, is exerting too much pressure on her metal. This pressure is aggravated by the strong fire in the girl's luck pillar as well as by the strong earth and fire she encountered in 1997. Earth is the resource element to metal, so it shows that the father's concern about his child, though of good intention, is excessive. If the earth is too heavy, it will bury the metal and suffocate it. This is exactly what too much attention can do to a child, leaving her no space to breathe and no room to develop her intelligence. The remedy is to allow the child more freedom to socialise with those of her own age, for example, by taking part in extracurricular activities.

Peering into the future, the girl will encounter good fortune after the age of 27 when she enters consecutive luck pillars of favourable wood and water. She will develop a successful business career as wood is her money and water her talent and skill. Her childhood, however, has too much earth and fire so her parents should not expect her to achieve brilliant results in school. She is, after all, neither naughty nor rebellious as such elements are not present. She does not need further disciplining from parents or teachers. All she needs is an opportunity to become more independent and more freedom to express her own ideas. Knowing that her daughter had a good future ahead calmed the mother and she agreed to follow my recommendations to improve her relationship with her daughter.

The resource element in our set of Four Pillars of Destiny symbolises our education, knowledge, thoughts, beliefs and conservatism. However this element is always in conflict with our aggression, as symbolised by our intelligence element. For example, for a metal person, his resource is earth which gives birth to metal, while his intelligence is water which the metal gives birth to. Earth destroys water, so resources and conservatism restraint intelligence and aggression. It is therefore necessary to strike a balance between these two important elements in our destiny. In our example, we have seen the danger of having too much resource element. It makes a person inert, lazy and too conservative.

Tragedy in the Making

Let us now examine the other extreme when a boy has too much intelligence element but lacks the resource element.

HOUR	DAY	MONTH	YEAR
癸 Water	丙 Fire	丙 Fire	戊 Earth
巳 Fire	辰 Earth	辰 Earth	午 Fire

54	44	34	24	14	4
壬 Water	辛 Metal	庚 Metal	己 Earth	戊 Earth	丁 Fire
戊 Earth	酉 Metal	申 Metal	未 Earth	午 Fire	巳 Fire

The Pillars of Destiny of a boy murderer

These Four Pillars belong to a boy of fire. There are plenty of earth elements but wood is totally absent. As fire gives birth to earth, earth is his intelligence element. Wood is his resource element. The fire self, exhausted by the multiple earth elements, is quite weak. His favourable elements are wood and fire while unfavourable elements are metal and earth. Water gives birth to a favourable element, wood. It is favourable when there is wood, but is not very helpful in this case as there is no wood for the water to support. Wood is very important to this child as it not only offers support and nutrition to his fire, but also helps keep the earth under control. Unfortunately there is no wood resources so the earth intelligence element is in danger of running berserk. The intelligence element, when uncontrolled, causes aggression to the point of rebelliousness. This danger exploded in 1993 when the boy, then 15 and in the luck pillar of strong earth, murdered his entire family, killing his father, mother, brothers and sisters in one horrifying night.

Having too much intelligence element without the resource element to counterbalance it could signify that the child is intelligent but rebellious. Such children need more discipline and attention from their parents. The discipline element is the same as the power and status element. It is the element that destroys and controls the self. And it is the element that can generate the resource element to keep the intelligence element under control. In our example of the fire boy murderer, his discipline or power element is water and water gives birth to wood – his resource element.

The following diagrams show the familiar Cycle of Birth and Cycle of Destruction, but in a different form. Instead of just showing the elements, they also show the five major aspects of life – money, power, intelligence, resources and colleagues – so that readers can better understand their relationships. Assuming the self is a wood person, let us examine his aspects of life:

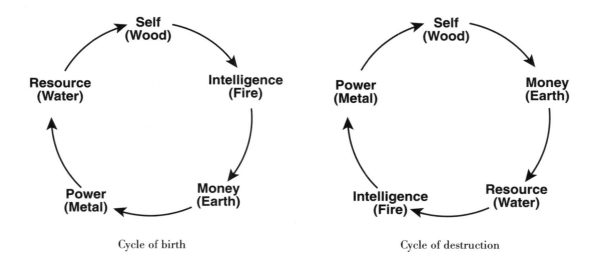

Cycle of birth   Cycle of destruction

Monica Seles – Tennis Prodigy

There are many striking examples of how a good balance of intelligence and resource elements can lead to success at a young age. The following pillars belong to Ms Monica Seles, the talented tennis queen who dominated the game as a teenager.

HOUR	DAY	MONTH	YEAR
?	壬 Water	癸 Water	癸 Water
?	申 Metal	亥 Water	丑 Earth

62	52	42	32	22	12	2
庚 Metal	己 Earth	戊 Earth	丁 Fire	丙 Fire	乙 Wood	甲 Wood
午 Fire	巳 Fire	辰 Earth	卯 Wood	寅 Wood	丑 Earth	子 Water

The Pillars of Destiny of Ms Monica Seles

She is a strong water lady whose abundant water is supported by metal, her resource element. She badly needs wood, her intelligence element, as an outlet for her water energy. This wood appears prominently in her luck pillars. Since the age of 2, she has enjoyed a strong wood influence which allowed her to channel her considerable water energy into tennis, chalking up great victories along the way. After the age of 22, both wood and fire become very strong. Fire represents her money so she will continue to enjoy both fame and fortune for many years to come.

The Richest Man in America

Mr Bill Gates is another excellent example of a destiny with balanced resource and intelligence elements. He is a water person born with plenty of earth elements in his destiny. Earth destroys water and is the power and status element to water. With so much earth, the water is weak and needs support from the resource element of metal in his hour pillar. This metal is crucial because the strong earth elements will channel their energy to support the metal and the metal can then support the water self. Without this resource element, the earth will focus on suppressing the water. In the heavenly stems of Mr Gates' year and month pillars, we also find wood, symbolising his intelligence, and fire, symbolising his money. Both these elements exhaust his water energy. Therefore, the water is still weak and needs support from metal.

HOUR	DAY	MONTH	YEAR
庚 Metal	壬 Water	丙 Fire	乙 Wood
戊 Earth	戊 Earth	戊 Earth	未 Earth

66	56	46	36	26	16	6
己 Earth	庚 Metal	辛 Metal	壬 Water	癸 Water	甲 Wood	乙 Wood
卯 Wood	辰 Earth	巳 Fire	午 Fire	未 Earth	申 Metal	酉 Metal

The Pillars of Destiny of Mr Bill Gates

Mr Gates' first two luck pillars from age 6 to 26 are wood and metal, symbolising his intelligence and resources. So he began demonstrating his immense talent with computers early in life. His great successes in business, however, only arrived after he reached his luck pillar of 36, the luck pillar of water over fire. Fire symbolises wealth to a water person and it was during this period that he become the richest man in the United States.

Mr Gates' success was brought about by the metal resource element in his hour pillar which is fully supported by the four earth elements in his earthly branches. This metal provided sufficient resources to his water self, enabling him to use his intelligence (wood) to produce his money (fire).

A superficial analysis of his Four Pillars gives the impression that he is strong in power and status (earth) but less so in money (fire). Unlike tycoons such as Mr Li-Ka-shing, his money element is not as prominent. This is because Mr Gates is not an out-and-out financier or speculator. His business is technology, and so his image is more that of an industrialist than a money man.

He has, however, plenty of money in his destiny. These are found in his three earth elements in the earthly branches of his month, day and hour pillars. The earthly branch of earth is in reality more complicated than the earthly branches of other elements. Earth represents mother earth and our mother earth contains everything. More advanced destiny techniques reveal that the earth 'dog' contains not only earth, but also metal and fire. So the three earth dogs also contain resources and money for Mr Gates. The earth dog, in our system, is called the storage of fire. This means Mr Gates' four pillars are standing on three rich storages of wealth. And this is why he is the richest man in the United States.

FENG SHUI

Feng Shui to Enhance Harmony

This book is not only about our family. Our home also plays an important role in our health and harmony so let us now spend some time on this topic. The Chinese metaphysical tool to deal with the home is called feng shui, a subject that is becoming very popular these days.

What is Feng Shui?

Feng shui is the study of our living environment. Traditionally, strong energies are believed to exist in our environment – the landscape, the water, the buildings, the roads and so on. Some energies are good and bring prosperity and good health to our lives. Others are bad and cause obstacles and misfortune. A good understanding of the nature of these energies and where they can be found enables us to choose a good location for our home, our bed, our desk and even our decorative objects. The Chinese believe that if everything is placed in accordance with feng shui principles, we can create a healthy, prosperous and harmonious environment and improve our quality of life.

The technique of the Four Pillars of Destiny is somewhat passive, in that the influences from the cycle of the five elements are beyond our control. Feng shui, on the other hand, is a tool we can control. Man is a mobile animal: We have the freedom to relocate ourselves from one place to another. If the feng shui energy of one location is not good, we can change or rearrange our home. Feng shui is, therefore, a positive tool we can employ to create a prosperous and harmonious environment at home.

'Feng shui' literally means wind and water in Chinese. The term seems to have been borrowed from an ancient Chinese classic called *Book of Burial* which provided guidelines for people to look for a prosperous spot of land to bury their ancestors. Certain spots called 'dragon's lairs' were believed to exist in the landscape. These are spots where the energy of the mountain, or the 'dragon', concentrates. It was believed that if our ancestors were buried in such spots, strong prosperity would be generated from the combination of the energy of man, earth and heaven. And such prosperity would be long lasting and would benefit future generations. A key sentence from this book defines what qualifies as a 'dragon's lair': "The energy of the dragon will be dissipated by wind and will stop at the boundary of water." The words, wind and water, now used to describe the subject of feng shui, are believed to have originated from this sentence.

The sentence appears simple but its meaning is of paramount importance to the subject of feng shui. It points out that energies exist in the 'dragon' – the landscape and the mountain ranges. The purpose of feng shui is to find a place in the landscape where there is a strong presence of this good energy. Such a place, a dragon's lair, must satisfy two main criteria. First, as the energy will be blown away by strong wind, the dragon's lair must be well-sheltered from strong wind. It must be protected on all sides. Second, the place must be close to a 'boundary of water'. This refers not only to physical flowing water, but also flat and open space.

It is easy to appreciate that good shelters are necessary to prevent energies from being blown away by wind. But the part about the 'boundary of water' requires a little bit of explanation. In feng shui, we compare mountains to dragons. Mountains can run continuously for thousands of miles and only stop when they arrive at the riverbank, the sea or a flat open space. Where they stop, the energy will also stop and stay in the open space or water boundary. If there is no water boundary, the mountain dragon will continue to run forward and carry away the energy as it runs. So the 'boundary of water' is a sign that the dragon has stopped and that the energy will stay.

The Fall of the Ming Dynasty

To appreciate the concept of a dragon's lair, let us examine the following sketch map of a famous tourist spot in China. This place is called the '13 Ming Tombs' and is the burial site for 13 emperors of the Ming dynasty. The tomb of the first emperor buried here is found in the upper right corner of the map. This location is well protected by the mountains on all sides and a lake is situated right in front of the tomb. Thus this site meets the criteria for a dragon's den well – it is sheltered from wind and there is a boundary of water helping the good energy to stay and concentrate.

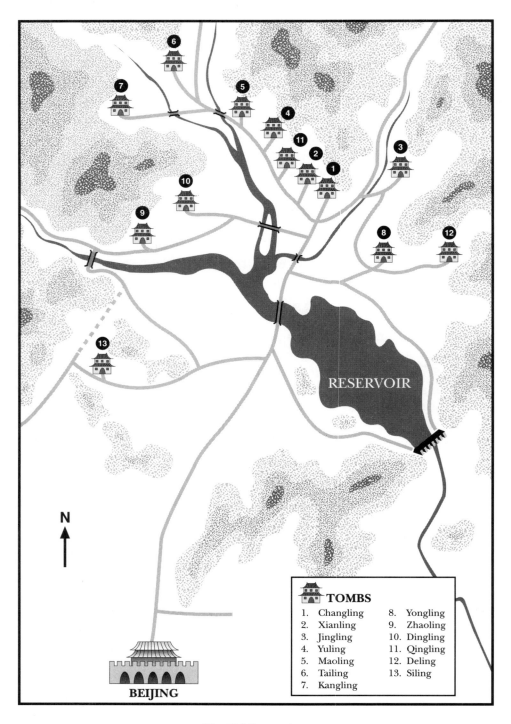

The 13 Ming tombs

TOMBS

1. Changling
2. Xianling
3. Jingling
4. Yuling
5. Maoling
6. Tailing
7. Kangling
8. Yongling
9. Zhaoling
10. Dingling
11. Qingling
12. Deling
13. Siling

But why then did the dynasty not prosper forever if the Ming emperors are buried in such good feng shui land? The Ming royal family eventually lost the country to the Manchurians from the north. History books offer many reasons for the decline of this prosperous dynasty. But from a metaphysical point of view, there are two reasons. First, although the location of the burial grounds of the earlier emperors are prosperous dragon's lairs, the later emperors were buried further and further away from the main spot. The tombs of the last few had totally deviated from the original site and their locations no longer qualified as dragon's lairs. The last Ming emperor was buried in the site in the bottom left corner of the map.

Second, the dragon's lair is only the physical configuration of the landscape. If we found such a spot, we would only have accomplished half of the feng shui task. As mentioned earlier, feng shui is also about the influence of the abstract energies or natural forces that exist in the environment. Even if we have found a dragon's lair, we must still ensure that the place can receive the most prosperous energy of the time. Such prosperous energy is dynamic and changes over time in a cyclical manner. As time passes, the prosperity of such energy will fade away. Therefore, no matter how perfect the physical environment of a grave site or building, its prosperity is never eternal.

In the old days, a feng shui expert had to go up the mountain to search for a dragon's lair. After such a lair was located, he would then determine the best direction to place the coffin and set up the tombstone. As mentioned earlier, strong prosperity will only be generated when there is the right mix of the energy of man (represented by the body of the ancestor), the energy of earth (which is rich in the dragon's lair), and the prosperous energy from heaven (as determined by the direction of the tombstone).

So selecting a good feng shui spot is not just about choosing a good physical environment – it also requires a thorough understanding of the energy from heaven. This then leads us to the fascinating body of knowledge called the 'flying stars'. The 'flying stars' is a technical term for the various energies in our surroundings. These energies are abstract and thus invisible to our eyes, but are believed to be closely associated with time and space. This means the energies are dynamic – they change continuously over time and move in space, affecting our wellbeing from different directions.

Through many thousands of years of study, the Chinese inherited a rich store of knowledge about these flying stars and discovered a formula to calculate the changing pattern of these stars over time. To understand the nature of the flying stars, we must go deeper into the philosophy of Chinese metaphysics. In the following chapters, I will take readers through the history of the flying stars and demonstrate how these theories can be applied in the designing of modern buildings.

How the Flying Stars Affect Us

Whether we are evaluating the feng shui of a site to bury our ancestors or to build a home, two aspects must be considered. These aspects – the physical surroundings and the abstract energies (or flying stars) – are like the hardware and the software of a computer; they are vitally interdependent.

For example, if someone decides to build a tall tower next to your house, is this good or bad? You cannot tell by looking at the shape of the tower alone. But if you understand the nature of the abstract forces acting at the location of the tower, you can deduce a great deal more about the impact of this tower on your house. Important questions can then be answered. Questions such as, will it cause good or bad influences? When will this influence happen? Who is likely to be affected? What can you do to enhance the influence if it is good, or to avoid the influence if it is bad? So feng shui is, in fact, the power of the abstract energies combining with the physical surroundings. If any part of the required information is not known, there cannot be any meaningful feng shui assessment.

Physical surroundings refer to all the objects we can see and feel in our environment, such as the landscape, mountains, water, buildings, roads and even the interior layout of a house and its decorative objects. But what are abstract forces? The Chinese first uncovered their characteristics many centuries ago. These forces are related to time and space, meaning they change over time and their impact comes from different directions. They can also be defined according to the five basic elements – metal, wood, water, fire and earth – which we have thoroughly described at the beginning of this book. So these forces are also governed by the principle of yin and yang and the cycles of birth and destruction of the five elements. But the most important discovery about these forces is that they change over time in a fixed and predictable pattern. This allows us to forecast the arrival of any good or bad feng shui influence and predict changes that will occur to our environment in the future.

The Origin of the Flying Stars

The concept of the flying stars in feng shui is derived from the large collection of ancient and complex Chinese wisdom, including the principle of yin and yang, the I Ching Trigrams, the theory of the five elements, and mysterious illustrations such as the Lo Shu diagram. These philosophies are well-known in Chinese culture and deserve extensive study. However, it is beyond the scope of this book to delve into this great store of knowledge in detail. Readers can look up my other books, such *Feng Shui and Destiny for Managers*, if they wish to learn more. In this chapter, I will only provide a basic idea of how these philosophies linked up to produce a solid foundation from which the flying star feng shui system developed.

These theories give us an overview of the history of the Universe, from the emergence of the basic forces and mechanisms that led to the formation of matter to the appearance of man and our understanding of nature through mathematics.

First the concept of yin and yang (the positive and negative duality of matter) hints of the origin of the Universe. Taoists believe that in the beginning, there was only a state of nothingness called *mu chi*. The splitting of this *mu chi* into yin and yang (called *tai chi*) began the Universe. The second phase was the appearance of the five basic elements interacting with one another to bring about cycles, changes, matter and life. Matter was formed from these elements, creating landscapes and natural phenomenon symbolised by the eight I Ching Trigrams in a configuration called the 'Early Arrangement'.

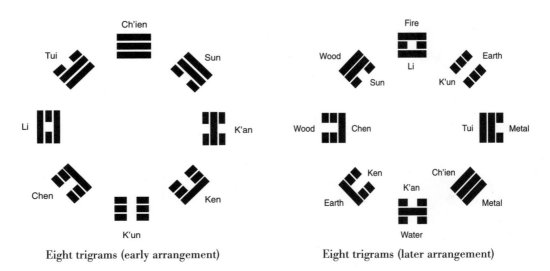

Eight trigrams (early arrangement)   Eight trigrams (later arrangement)

Number	Trigram	Element	Nature	Person	Age
1	☵	Water	Water	Middle-aged man	1
2	☷	Earth	Earth	Old woman	2
3	☳	Wood	Thunder	Eldest son	3
4	☴	Wood	Wind	Eldest daughter	4
5	—	Earth	—	—	5
6	☰	Metal	Heaven	Old man	6
7	☱	Metal	Swamp	Young girl	7
8	☶	Earth	Mountain	Young boy	8
9	☲	Fire	Fire	Middle-aged woman	9

The meaning of the trigrams

The trigrams were later rearranged by an emperor of the Chou dynasty into a new order called the 'Later Arrangement' to encompass more complex matters such as human relationships. As civilisations prospered and knowledge grew, the trigrams were expanded into 64 hexagrams to embrace more meanings and contexts. Man also developed a strong appetite to understand nature through science and mathematics. These stages are also reflected in the Lo Shu, a mysterious diagram with dots arranged in an unusual pattern. According to Chinese legend, this diagram was found on the back of a giant tortoise which emerged from the Lo River in central China about 6,000 years ago.

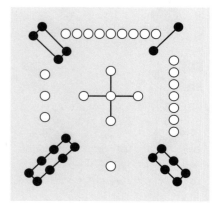

The Lo Shu diagram

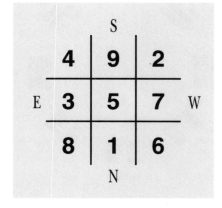

The original nine square chart

The arrangement of the dots on the tortoise shell, when translated into numbers, gives us a tool called the 'nine square chart' showing a unique configuration of numbers in a fixed pattern. This pattern is believed to reveal the movement of the flying stars through time and space.

The Concept of Time

To encompass the experience of time, the Chinese also established a cyclical concept of counting time in 180-year cycles. This is the concept of the 'Three Periods and Nine Ages'.

The following diagram shows how a cycle of 180 years can be divided into three Periods of 60 years each and then subdivided into 20-year Ages. Each 20-year Age is marked with a number from one to nine, and these numbers carry the meaning of the I Ching Trigram.

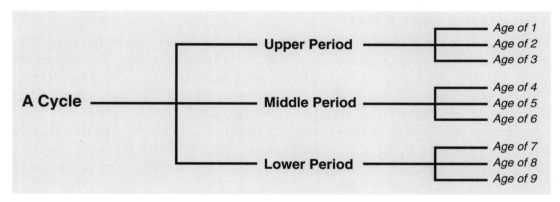

The Three Periods and Nine Ages

With this system of counting, the abstract concept of time comes alive, with meanings assigned to it by the trigrams. For example, the 'Age of Seven' refers to the female trigram 'tui', which also symbolises the human mouth. These qualities cast a strong influence on our society during the Age of Seven (1984 to 2004). Since 1984, we have witnessed numerous female leaders rising to power, including Margaret Thatcher, Cory Aquino, Madeleine Albright and Anson Chan. The world has also seen great advances in information technology and communication techniques such as the Internet, which are related to the human mouth.

We can thus trace the development of the Universe through these ancient theories. Though simplified, the Chinese cosmic model is strikingly similar to modern cosmology developed separately through Western sciences. The 'Big Bang theory' popular in the West depicts the origin of the Universe as a state of singularity with all matter concentrated within a spot of infinite density before the cosmic explosion. This state and the evolution of the elements and matter after the Big Bang resemble the idea of the *mu chi* developing into the *tai chi* and the five basic elements. The different branches of Chinese metaphysics, including flying star feng shui, are derived from this Chinese cosmic model.

The yin and yang and the five elements provide an understanding of the basic forces interacting in the Universe. The I Ching Trigrams assemble all matters in the Universe in simple symbolic form. The Lo Shu diagram simulates an understanding of space and mathematics. And the concept of the 'Three Periods and Nine Ages' provides a measuring rod for the passage of time. By combining all these concepts, we can derive a compact model of the natural forces acting on us at any time and space. This model is called the flying star chart and it is the tool that enables us to assess the different feng shui energies affecting the different locations of our home.

The Flying Star Chart

The flying star chart incorporates all the ancient theories mentioned here. The numbers are numerical expressions of the trigrams so they carry the meanings of the five elements, the yin and yang, as well as symbolise various matters in the Universe. Each of the nine squares represents a direction, thus incorporating the concept of space. These numbers are not static as they move over time according to the fixed pattern indicated in the Lo Shu diagram. The deceptively simple nine square flying star chart is thus a very effective model of the feng shui energies, capable of showing the various natural forces affecting any point in space at any moment of time.

This nine square chart is the trademark of the flying star school of feng shui. The nine squares represent the eight directions plus the centre. Traditionally the South has always been placed on top and the North at the bottom. The West is thus on the right and the East on the left. The squares in between these four cardinal points are Southwest, Northwest, Northeast and Southeast. The practice of placing the South on top may have originated from the idea that the flames of the fire, symbolising the south direction, rise upward while water, symbolising the north direction as shown in the Later Arrangement of the Eight Trigrams, flows downward.

The numbers in each square are called the flying stars. Flying stars refer to the abstract forces of nature coming from different directions. They are symbolised by numbers which originate from the trigrams. As the trigrams are a symbol of all matters in the Universe, so too are the numbers. If we understand the meaning of the numbers, we then can understand the nature of the flying stars affecting a certain direction or location of a house. The following table shows the basic meanings of the numbers 1 to 9.

No.	Trigram	Element	Person	Object	Body	Effects
1		Water	Middle-aged man	Den, Blood	Ear, Kidney	Academic Matters
2		Earth	Old woman	Earth, Ox	Nose, Stomach	Sickness
3		Wood	Eldest son	Thunder	Foot, Hair, Liver	Anger
4		Wood	Eldest daughter	Wind, Rope	Buttocks, Neck	Romance, Sex
5	—	Earth	—	Shar	—	Bad luck, Obstacles
6		Metal	Old man	Heaven	Head, Lungs	Past prosperity, Legal matters
7		Metal	Young girl	Lake	Mouth	Current prosperity
8		Earth	Young boy	Mountain	Hands	Coming prosperity
9		Fire	Middle-aged woman	Beauty	Eyes, Heart	Future prosperity

The meaning of the numbers in a flying star chart

This table shows the basic meanings of the numbers in a flying star chart. However, as the flying stars also have a time dimension, their meanings will also change with time. As a rule, the number of the prevailing Age is always the most prosperous number. The number of the immediate subsequent Age is the second most prosperous. Any number smaller than that of the current Age possesses only faded energy and so signifies unfavourable influence. For example, as we are now in the Age of Seven, 7 represents current prosperity. Eight is the second best number as it represents future prosperity. Nine is also favourable as it represents more distant prosperity. But any number smaller than 7, from 1 to 6, is unfavourable. This will change in 2004 when we enter the Age of Eight. For the 20 years between 2004 to 2024, 8 will be current prosperity, 9 future prosperity and 1 distant future prosperity. Seven becomes an unfavourable number.

When an Age changes, not only do the meanings of the numbers change, the positions of the flying stars change too. The original nine square chart has 5 in the centre. However, this only applies to the Age of Five. When we move to the Age of Seven, 7 replaces 5 in the centre square. All the other numbers then shift according to the pattern in the Lo Shu diagram. The flying star chart representing the Age of Seven is thus very different from the chart representing the Age of Five.

4	9	2
3	5	7
8	1	6

Original nine square chart

6	2	4
5	7	9
1	3	8

Age of Seven nine square chart

This new flying star chart, with 7 in the centre, shows the feng shui energies for an 'Age of Seven' building, that is, any building constructed between 1984 and 2004.

The flying stars are continuously shifting, just like the stars in the sky. The strength of the flying star school is that they realise and emphasise the time dimension in feng shui analysis. Feng shui influence is constantly changing with time, like everything else in the Universe. History proves that no feng shui influence can last forever because China has seen many powerful dynasties come and go over the centuries. These changes are brought about by the changing pattern of feng shui influence as reflected in the flying star chart.

The flying stars, as symbolised by the numbers in the nine square chart, are symbols of the natural forces related to time and space. The chart reflects the natural forces acting on the different parts of a building, house or apartment. With this chart, we can determine what energies are affecting the different sections of a house. We can identify which locations are receiving the prosperous energy and utilise this good energy by using the space for active functions. We can also identify which locations are getting the influence of bad energies and avoid sleeping in these places to minimise the unfavourable effect.

These theories may appear complicated initially but the flying star chart is not difficult to draw. With just a simple formula and two pieces of information – the orientation of the building and the Age when the building was completed, we can draw up a chart for any house. Detailed steps on how to construct a feng shui chart for a building can be found in Appendix 4.

Checking the Feng Shui
of Your Home

In the last two chapters, I have briefly introduced the feng shui technique to readers. Now let us see how an actual feng shui investigation is done. Say you are going to examine the feng shui of your home – a ground floor apartment. Before you start, you need some basic equipment. These include a Lo Pan, a pencil, an eraser, a ruler and a compass for drawing circles.

A Lo Pan is a Chinese compass specially designed for feng shui purposes. Its basic function is to measure accurately the directions of a building. Like any other compass, it has a magnetic needle in the centre. However, a Lo Pan not only indicates directions but also has complicated formulae to explain the implication of each direction. A typical good Lo Pan has a circular plate with beautifully engraved symbols, Chinese characters and I Ching trigrams and hexagrams. Don't be put off by its apparent complexity as most of the formulae are only used for yin house feng shui – the analysis of grave sites for the dead. For yang house feng shui, or the analysis of houses and buildings for the living, the most important ring of information is the 24 mountains.

The 24 mountains of the Lo Pan

The 24 mountains are markings of directions in a full circle of 360 degrees. Each section occupies 15 degrees. As Appendix 4 shows, different mountains have different flying star charts. Each direction must therefore be measured to an accuracy of at least 15 degrees as indicated by the 24 mountains on the Lo Pan.

As explained previously, two pieces of information are needed to draw up a flying star chart for a building. First, we need to find out the Age of the building, or the 20-year period within which the building was built and occupied. For example, a building completed in 1972 is an 'Age of Six' building while one completed in 1988 is an 'Age of Seven' building.

The second bit of essential information is the orientation or direction of the building. This is the direction the front of the building faces, which we must measure with a Lo Pan. But before we can do this, we must first determine the 'front' of the building.

In the past, when buildings were of regular rectangular shapes, with the main entrance always facing the main road, it was easy to identify the side with main entrance as the front. However, modern buildings have various shapes and the main entrance may not be at the front of the building. So we can no longer just take the side with the entrance as the front. We need to walk around the building and determine carefully where the intended front should be. To make such a decision, we can regard a building as a person who needs breathing space. The front of the building is like a person's face: there should be some open space in front of his nose so that he can breathe. Thus we sometimes look for such open space to identify the front. This could be the main road or the garden. Bear in mind, however, that the front should also be assessable from outside. If the sea lies behind your building and there is no entry from that direction, this side cannot be the front of the building despite the open space.

Using the Lo Pan

After examining the surroundings and identifying the front of the building, we can now use the Lo Pan to measure the direction. The magnetic needle housed in the small, round box (called the 'heaven's pool') in the centre of the Lo Pan is extremely sensitive and delicate. In the cities, many sources of magnetic distraction can affect the needle and give you a wrong reading. When you use the Lo Pan, stand in an open space, as far away as possible from any large objects. Parked cars, lamp posts, metal fences or even concrete structures can affect the needle. Keep at least a few metres away from such objects. More detailed instructions on how to use the Lo Pan and how to draw the flying star chart can be found in Appendix 4.

Once the direction of the building has been established and its Age ascertained, we can either construct the flying star chart using the steps in Appendix 4 or look up the relevant flying star chart in Appendix 5.

Let us assume that our building faces exact west and was completed and occupied in 1988. This makes it an 'Age of Seven' building. The following is the flying star chart of this building.

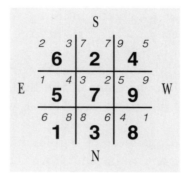

Flying star chart of building

The flying star chart is a nine square chart. Each square represents one direction. There are three numbers in each square. The larger number in the centre represents time, as it is derived from the Age of the building. This number is vital when constructing the chart, but less important subsequently when interpretation begins. The two smaller numbers represent the feng shui influences affecting the building in the location or direction covered by the square. For example, if we wish to examine the western part of the building, we only need to look at the pair of small numbers, 3 and 7, in the west square. The number on the right, 7, is called the 'water star'. It shows the money aspect of the direction. The number on the left, 3, is the 'mountain star'. It indicates aspects of human harmony, including health, relationships, power, authority and security. With the flying star chart, we can examine the money and human aspects of all locations in a building. The same flying star chart applies to any unit within the same building. You can even refer to the same chart when decorating a desk in the study of any apartment within the building.

When examining the water star and the mountain star in a flying star chart, we should first look for the prosperous stars. As explained in the last chapter, we are currently in the 'Age of Seven', so 7 means current prosperity, 8 future prosperity, and 9 the prosperity of the more distant future. Any number smaller than 7 belongs to the past and is not prosperous. The worst numbers in the chart are 2, 3 and 5 as these numbers have bad implications such as sickness, obstacles and agitation, as shown in the table in the previous chapter.

The flying stars are abstract energies. Readers, however, may recall that we need to examine both the physical environment and the abstract energy before we can make any sense out of feng shui. We must therefore observe the physical aspect of the apartment as well. Physical aspect means both the external and internal environment – buildings, mountains, roads, water in the surroundings, the interior design of the apartment, such as the shape of the floor plan, the different functions of the different rooms, and so on. The basic principles are:

- the prosperous water star should be placed in water while the prosperous mountain star should be placed on the mountain;
- water is active, open and fluid while the mountain is quiet, enclosed and stable.

All this may seem rather abstract but you will be able to appreciate its deeper meaning after studying the examples in this and the subsequent chapters.

Analysing the Feng Shui of Our Home

Let us now continue with our task of analysing the feng shui of our home. After working out the flying star chart, the next step is to obtain a floor plan of our unit. If a floor plan is not available, you should measure the interior dimensions and draw a sketch plan as accurately to scale as possible. The following is the floor plan of the apartment we are going to examine.

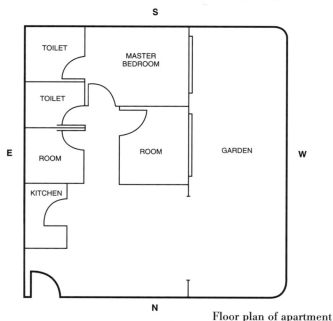

Floor plan of apartment

141

Locate the centre of the apartment on the floor plan and draw a circle. Then divide the circle into eight equal sectors so that we can see clearly which direction covers which part of the building.

We can now begin our interpretation. In a home, the most important places are the inlets of energy – the entrance and the windows – and the livingroom and the master bedroom. Let us examine these areas first.

The entrance to the apartment is located within the NE sector where the water star 6 and the mountain star 2 are found. As the entrance is an active spot, the water star 6 applies. The water star 6 implies legal trouble and so this is not a good entrance. However, the apartment has a garden in the W and NW and the livingroom has large windows and glass doors in these locations. The flying star chart shows that the water star 8 is found in the NW and the water star 7 in the W. The windows and the glass doors facing W and NW can thus receive the strong prosperous energy of the water star 8 and the water star 7, both of which symbolise good money aspects. As the window and glass door can let in more sunlight and energy than the entrance in the NE, the strong energy in the W and NW more than compensates for the drawback of the entrance. The livingroom is located in the NW and can receive the prosperous energy of the water star 8. This apartment is thus quite strong in money aspects.

Let us now examine the master bedroom. It is located in the SW sector where the mountain star 8 and the water star 3 reside. A bedroom is a quiet, enclosed place, so the mountain star applies. The mountain star 8 is prosperous and enhances health, harmony and stability for those living in this room. Hence the master bedroom is a good room.

Let us look at the other parts of the apartment. Room B in the W sector has the mountain star 3 and the water star 7. Number 7 is a good star but 3 is a bad one. If we use this room for sleeping, we will activate the mountain aspect of the room and support the bad energy of the number 3. But if we use this room for active functions, for example, as a study or play room, we can activate the prosperous water star 7. This room is best for active functions such as work, study or play.

Room C is located in the E where the strong mountain star 7, which is good for health and human harmony, resides. So this room is best used as a bedroom.

The kitchen is located in the NE with the water star 6 and the mountain star 2. The kitchen is an active place so the water star 6 applies. The water star 6 is not prosperous and belongs to the metal element. The kitchen is a place of the fire element as we use heat to cook. Fire destroys metal, so we can foresee this kitchen causing illness relating to metal. In a previous chapter, I have explained that metal is related to the breathing organs. As metal number 6 is being destroyed by fire in the kitchen, we can expect the occupants of the house to be more susceptible to health problems relating to the breathing organs. This may particularly affect the father, as the number 6 is a symbol of the trigram meaning heaven and father.

We now have a general view of the feng shui of our apartment and the prosperity of each room. The final phase is to recommend the placement of furniture and decorative objects to enhance the good energy and minimise the damage of the bad energy. Let me briefly show readers how this is done.

If we have identified a prosperous water star 7, 8 or 9 in a certain location within our apartment, we should activate such good energy. The best way to do this is to use the location for active functions, for example, as a play room or livingroom, and to place active, moving objects there to generate strong energy. As the good water energy of 7 and 8 is found in the livingroom, we should place active objects such as a hi-fi system, TV set or telephone in this prosperous area. We can also place rotating objects like a clock. Even a fish tank with colourful fish is an active object which can generate prosperous energy if put in the right place. We can also place a mirror on the wall opposite the prosperous energy area. Just as a mirror can draw in the images of objects on the opposite side, it can also draw good energy deeper into the livingroom. The sofa in the livingroom should also be placed such that the occupants can sit with their faces greeting the prosperous water star in the W and NW.

As for the master bedroom, the flying star chart shows that the strong mountain star 8 is in the SW. The best place for the bed is thus in the SW so that the occupants can sleep with their heads well supported by the good mountain star 8. This will enhance harmony and health in the bedroom.

This is an example of how we can use the flying star chart to check the feng shui of our house. First we identify the prosperous water star and mountain star locations. After that we can choose an appropriate interior design to enhance both money prosperity and human health and harmony at home.

Disharmony from Bad Feng Shui

The apartment we analysed in the last chapter has reasonably good feng shui with money prosperity as well as human harmony. The family members who live in the house have enjoyed career advancement, rising social status and good household harmony. The husband has managed to expand his business overseas while the wife was awarded a Badge of Honour by the Queen for services to the community. The children are well behaved and have done reasonably well in school. The house exudes a comfortable atmosphere and even the pet dog is friendly and healthy! However, not all homes enjoy such good feng shui. In this chapter and the next, I will show readers examples where bad feng shui brought misfortune and tragedy.

Our home is our castle where we can recuperate from the daily stress of the outside world and be ourselves. So when analysing the feng shui of our home, the aspect of human harmony is even more important than money prosperity. The key to human harmony in the house is the mountain stars. A good mountain star must be placed on a mountain. The mountain stars 7, 8 or 9 should be well enclosed in a quiet room, such as the master bedroom or other bedroom. If these good mountain stars fall into active places such as the livingroom, entrance, study, kitchen or toilet, such a configuration is known as 'mountain star falls in water'. This is bad for human harmony in the house.

Let us examine the following example where a home's main entrance, the mountain star 7 and the water star 3 are all located in the W. As the entrance is an active position, the water star 3 takes effect. The water star 3 is a bad star that symbolises agitation and anger. The good mountain star 7 also falls in water at the entrance. The mountain star 7 is a good mountain star that should be placed in a quiet and enclosed area. If you put it at the entrance, the activity of the entrance will destroy the mountain star and badly disrupt human harmony in the house. The number 7 is also a symbol of a young girl. If a young girl lives in the house, her parents will likely find her rebellious and hard to live with.

A Suicide in Hong Kong

The following is a real-life example of a tragedy brought about by a good mountain star falling in water. This tragedy occurred in the home of a French expatriate in Hong Kong. Four persons lived in the apartment: a French gentleman, his wife, their 21-year-old daughter and a Filipino domestic helper. In August 1995, the French couple returned to Paris for a holiday, leaving their daughter and Filipino maid in the house. Early one morning, the young lady asked the maid to buy some food from the market. When the maid returned, she was shocked to find that the young lady had fallen 13 stories onto the podium of the building. She was rushed to hospital but was proclaimed dead on arrival. The police later found a short handwritten note bidding farewell to her parents and the case was deemed a suicide.

I do not know much about the events leading to the tragedy but on checking the feng shui of the apartment at the request of the landlord, it was obvious that this home did not enjoy good human harmony. The following is a sketch of the floor plan of this unusually-shaped apartment. The apartment may have been formed from two adjoining symmetrical apartments.

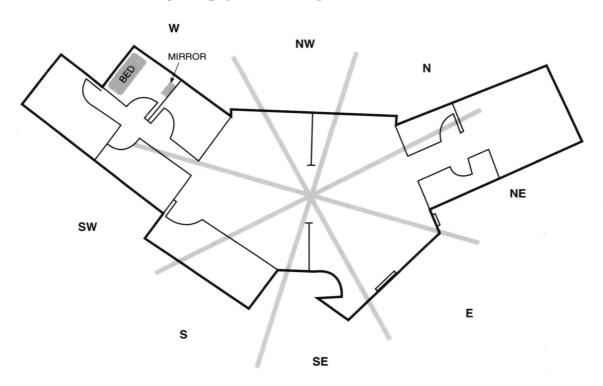

Floor plan of the apartment where the lady committed suicide

This 'Age of Six' building has its front facing SW and its back against NE. With this information we can draw up the flying star chart:

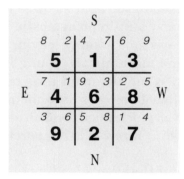

Flying star chart of the apartment

If we divide the floor plan into eight sectors showing the eight major directions, we can immediately see where the flying stars are located in the apartment. Let us start with the entrance. The main door is located in the SE, and the flying star chart shows the mountain star 8 and the water star 2 in this sector. As the door is an active position, the water star 2 is the one that matters. The water star 2 is a bad star symbolising sickness. This alone reveals it to be a bad entrance. With the mountain star 8 also at the entrance, thus 'placing the mountain star in water', the good mountain star is destroyed, signifying the destruction of human harmony.

Moving on to the livingroom, we arrive at the E sector where the mountain star 7 and the water star 1 reside. The livingroom is an active position, so finding the prosperous mountain star 7 here is again another sign of poor human aspects as the mountain star 7 is destroyed when placed in an active position.

There are only three good mountain stars in the chart. As we have seen, both the 7 and 8 have been destroyed. We thus have to look to the mountain star 9 for remedy. Unfortunately, the mountain star 9 is found in the centre of the chart. The centre of the house is the centre of the livingroom, a very active place that links the two sides of the livingroom. So the remaining good mountain star 9 is also destroyed by the activity. We can therefore conclude that human harmony is very poor in the house and this perhaps caused the tragedy.

Let us also look at other major areas in the apartment. The master bedroom is in the NE where the flying star chart shows the presence of the mountain star 3, a bad star representing anger and agitation.

The worst location may well be in the W, where the mountain star 2 and the water star 5 are found. Of the nine numbers, the worst are 2 and 5 and misfortune doubles when these two bad numbers fall in same location, reinforcing each other. We thus expect misfortune to occur in the W of the apartment. And indeed this small room in the W was the bedroom of the young French lady.

The Image of a Fox

I also noticed something bizarre. The Frenchman was apparently an enthusiastic collector of Oriental antiques and handicraft and owned a number of fox figures in his collection. On one side of the livingroom wall was a contemporary painting of the face of a cunning and ugly fox. This picture directly faced the balcony where the lady jumped to her death.

Traditionally the fox is believed to be an inauspicious animal. In Chinese legends, the fox is sometimes depicted as a reincarnation of those who practised witchcraft or black magic to gain longevity, but failed. Examine the shape of the floor plan again. Does it not resemble the face of a fox …

The multiple images of the fox add to the mystery of the lady's death. Perhaps the bad feng shui created an environment suitable for some malicious spiritual forces? One last observation worth noting is that the French lady had placed a mirror directly opposite her bed. This is taboo in feng shui. We will talk more about the placement of furniture and decorative objects in subsequent chapters.

Troubled Houses

The secret to good flying star feng shui is ensuring the right allocation of mountain stars and water stars in our environment. If these stars are suitably placed, with the good mountain stars enclosed in a mountain position and the good water stars opened up in a water position, we can generate strong human harmony and money prosperity.

In the last example, we saw how the wrong allocation of the mountain stars caused poor human relationships that led to the tragic death of a young lady. In this chapter, I will introduce more examples to show how a good understanding of the flying stars can help explain events in our house.

House of Legal Trouble

The following is the floor plan of an Age of Six two-storey house with a large garden and beautiful seaview at the back in Discovery Bay, Hong Kong.

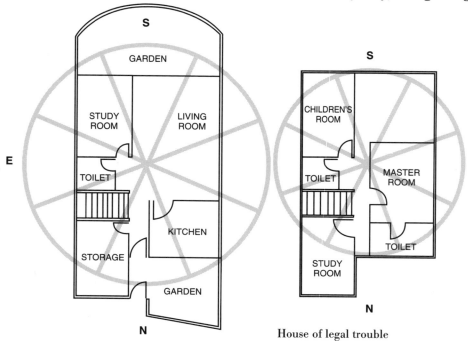

House of legal trouble

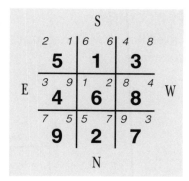

Flying star chart

The main entrance is in the N. In the S is a large garden with the open sea beyond. The flying star chart shows that the water star 7 is in the N, right at the entrance. So the entrance is a prosperous one. But after entering the house, a narrow passageway runs through the kitchen, work area and toilets before reaching the livingroom. A water star 7 must be activated with open space. The best position for this prosperous star is an active, fluid and open area, with as few obstructions and partitions as possible. However, the design of this house does not meet this requirement. The narrow passage with many rooms and partitions greatly reduces the benefit of the prosperous water star 7. On the other hand, the S sector where the livingroom, the garden and the open sea are is open and spacious. This environment will certainly generate strong prosperity if a strong water star such as 7 or 8 is present here. Unfortunately, the S sector is occupied by a pair of 6s, which indicate faded prosperity and legal trouble. This water star 6 is strong as it is supported by the vast open space of the garden and the sea.

Let us now go upstairs and check the bedrooms. The master bedroom is found in the NW and W, where the mountain stars 8 and 9 are located. This is a good room that enhances human harmony. The children's room, however, is located in the SE and E where the mountain stars 2 and 3, both bad stars, reside. With the negative impact of the water star 6 in the livingroom and the garden, and the bad mountain stars in the children's room, we can expect some misfortune to befall the children. And indeed, the teenage son living in the room was charged with possession of illegal drugs.

House of Unhappy Marriage

The next example demonstrates how the flying stars bring about the Flower of Romance and an unhappy marriage.

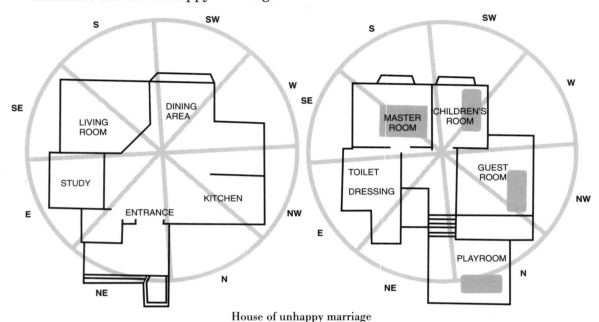

House of unhappy marriage

Flying star chart

This is a luxurious house with gardens and a fish pond. The house was built in the Age of Seven with its front facing NE and back against SW. The entrance is located in the NE. The flying star chart reveals that the water star 4, signifying sex and romance, is at the entrance. A water fountain in the shape of a fish with open mouth can be found right at the entrance. This active water generates strong support for the water star 4, so we can expect the romance aspect in this house to be strong. However, as 4 is a bad star belonging to the prosperity of the past, activating this star means romance in the negative sense, or even a scandal.

Nevertheless, the house is not all bad. The strong water star 7 is found in the SW where the dining room, which has large windows opening to the spacious back garden, is located. The water star 7 is thus able to generate strong money prosperity. The good water star 8 found in the study and livingroom also produces money prosperity. But when we walk outside the house, we find drawbacks. The large fish pond in the garden extends from the N sector, passing the NW of the house and ends at the W sector. The pond has many energetic fish which will activate the water stars in these three sectors. Unfortunately, the water stars are 6, 2 and 3. None of these is prosperous. Another negative aspect is that in the N sector the good mountain star 8 falls in water, and this is bad for human harmony.

The second floor has three main rooms. The playroom is in the N, occupying the sector of the mountain star 8 and the water star 6. A good mountain star needs a quiet and enclosed environment to enhance its strength. Placing the mountain star 8 in a playroom does not help human harmony. This room is best used for sleeping.

The master bedroom occupies the SE and S. The S sector is fine with the good mountain star 9 but the worst mountain star of 5 is found in the SE. Unfortunately, the owner of the house placed his large bed in the SE under the strong influence of this mountain star 5. He also placed a large mirror on the SE wall just behind his bed. So the location and the placement of furniture made this room the worst in the house. The children's room in the SW is an excellent one with the mountain star 7 but this room was left empty.

With these feng shui observations, we can now predict the fate of the occupant of this house. The household consists of a single gentleman, living alone. The man did rather well in business but failed badly in his married life. He had frequent romances and married three times. None of the marriages, however, lasted more than two years. And so, at the age of 50, he remained single.

This sad state of affairs matches the feng shui of the house. But if you understand the root of the problem, it is not difficult to offer solutions and remedies. The following were my major recommendations:

- The water fountain at the entrance should be demolished;
- The fish pond occupying the N, NW and W sectors should be filled up;
- The master bedroom and the children's room should be merged into one large room with the bed placed in the SW sector;
- The playroom should be converted into a second bedroom.

These recommendations were happily accepted by my client and he turned the fish pond into a mini golf course.

Interior Design for Harmony

In the previous chapters, I have emphasised more than once that when analysing the feng shui of a house, both the physical environment as well as the abstract energy – the flying stars – must be considered. After studying several cases, readers should by now be able to appreciate that even the flying stars need the support of the appropriate physical environment to deliver their beneficial or adverse influences. The physical environment thus plays a very important role in feng shui analysis. Let us now leave aside the flying stars for the time being and devote our attention to the physical environment in the home.

The term physical environment covers a wide area. It actually refers to any object we can see with our eyes. Mountains, water, the landscape, buildings, roads, the shapes of objects, floor plans, the interior allocation of space, the placement of furniture, decorative objects: all these fall within this category. Readers can find detailed descriptions of some external physical structures which can affect the feng shui of an environment in my book *Feng Shui and Destiny for Managers*. Here, I intend to concentrate on the placement of furniture and decorative objects in the home.

Twenty Common Errors

The following is a floor plan I prepared for the Hong Kong Health and Fortune Expo 1997, organised by the Hong Kong Tourist Association. This plan represents a typical apartment in Hong Kong and on it I indicated 20 common mistakes in interior decoration and placement of furniture. These errors are traditionally considered bad feng shui and can create disharmony or discomfort in the home. If combined with the arrival of a bad flying star in the location, it may bring about obstacles or misfortune. Each of these errors and their bad implications are explained below:

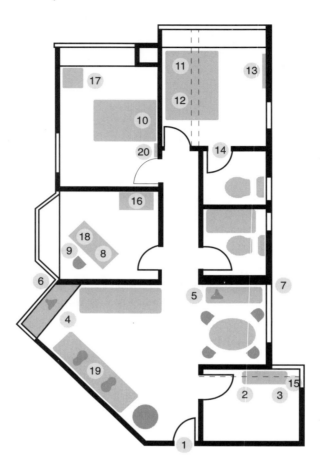

Wrong interior arrangement

1. Wooden arrow

This is an unfavourable influence created by a long passageway between the entrance and the bedroom door. The long, straight passage generates a strong and direct rush of 'chi' (feng shui energies). As a long object is classified as the wood element in feng shui, this is called a 'wooden arrow'.

One remedy is to construct a curved door at the entrance to the passageway. Rounded objects are classified as metal and so help keep the wooden arrow under control.

2. Exposed stove

Traditionally the stove is a source of prosperous energy that is personal to a family. Placing the stove in an exposed location reduces its beneficial power.

The stove thus should not be placed where it can be immediately seen by visitors entering the house.

3. Stove facing outward

If the stove is placed with the knobs facing outward of the house, its prosperous energy will be driven outside.

Place the stove such that the knobs face inward into the house.

4. Religious statue with back against window

Placing religious statues against the window creates an image of insecurity and instability.

Religious statues should be placed with their back against a solid wall to symbolise strength and stability.

5. White tiger opening mouth

The left side of a religious statue is traditionally called the 'green dragon side' while the right side is called the 'white tiger side'. An opening such as a window or entrance immediately adjacent to the right side of a statue is unfavourable as it symbolises a white tiger opening its mouth to harm people.

Remedy: Leave some wall space on the right side of the religious statue.

6. & 7. Leakage of 'chi'

After coming in through the entrance, the feng shui energies, or 'chi', are usually drawn towards the two opposite corners before bouncing back and circulating around the house. But if these two corners are windows, the energies will escape through the windows instead of circulating in the house, thus causing a 'leakage' of beneficial energy.

If there is no wall space at the window corners to enable the energy to stay and circulate, put up curtains and plants at these corners to create some shelter.

8. Desk directly facing the entrance

The entrance is where energies rush in. Placing a desk to face the entrance directly is thus inappropriate.

The best desk position is at the diagonally opposite corner of the room.

9. Back against the corner

Desks should not be placed at an angle to the walls. Not allowing the desk to lean against a wall creates an image of insecurity, like 'floating on air'. Moreover, placing oneself against the corner symbolises diminishing business just as the space diminishes towards the corner.

The best desk position is to lean against the wall at a right angle to one side. This way, a person can sit with his back against a solid wall.

10. Bed with back towards the entrance

If the entrance is behind the head of the bed, the sleeping person will not be able to see anyone entering the room. This creates an atmosphere of insecurity.

The best position for a bed is similar to that for a desk, with the bed leaning against the corner to form a diagonal with the entrance.

11. Overhead beam

Sitting or sleeping directly beneath a heavy overhead beam is believed to be harmful as this creates pressure on the person below. Avoid placing yourself directly underneath a beam. If this is inevitable, construct a false ceiling to hide the beam.

12. Bed facing the entrance directly

When the bed, the passageway and the entrance are in a straight line, a current of energies will rush directly towards the bed. A bed facing the entrance also lacks privacy.

Avoid placing the bed to face the entrance.

13. Mirror facing the bed

A mirror facing the bed reflects the image of the sleeping person. Traditionally the mirror image is believed to represent the 'yin' aspect of a person and exposing it for a long period is harmful. The sleeping person may also be frightened by his own image when he wakes up in the dark.

When placing a mirror in the bedroom, avoid having it face the bed.

14. Toilet facing the bed

The toilet is considered a 'dirty' part of the house with bad energy. So having the bed face the toilet is unhealthy.

Most master bedrooms in modern condominiums have this drawback. If this cannot be avoided, shut the toilet door when sleeping.

15. Beam above the stove

The stove is especially important to the wife. Placing the stove beneath a heavy concrete beam can thus adversely affect the wife's health.

Avoid placing the stove beneath a heavy beam.

16. Sharp edges

When placing two desks, the corner of one desk may inadvertently point directly at the other desk like an arrow aimed at a person. This creates a menacing atmosphere.

Avoid such 'sharp' positions when making desk arrangements.

17. Scissors

This describes a situation where the sharp corners of two pieces of furniture point towards each other. Besides being a safety hazard, this also creates disharmony and hostility.

Avoid such 'scissors' configurations when placing your furniture.

18. Desk floating on air

A desk that is placed without touching or leaning against a wall symbolises insecurity and instability.

A better arrangement is to lean the desk against the wall on one side while the person sits with his back against another wall.

19. Lions' wrath

Lions are fierce animals and lion statues are normally placed outside the house to protect the prosperity. Placing fierce lion statues indoors, facing family members, is inappropriate. Statues of more serene animals, like the tortoise, the unicorn or the elephant, are more suitable inside the home.

20. Mirror facing windows

A mirror reflects objects on the opposite side. If a mirror faces the window, it can draw the image of any object outside into the house. If these are unpleasant objects, they may bring harm to the family.

We should thus avoid placing a mirror to face the window.

Now that we have looked at these common errors, let us rearrange our furniture to put the 20 items in proper feng shui order. The following is the same floor plan with everything in order:

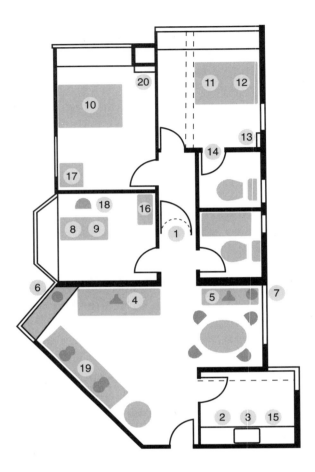

Correct interior arrangement

Although feng shui is not merely about eye-pleasing decorations, most of its principles run parallel with comfort, safety, hygiene and the appropriate use of space in a modern home design. The ultimate goal of feng shui design is to create a comfortable, prosperous, healthy and harmonious environment. It is not just about the invisible flying stars – visual comfort is also vital. I believe the best feng shui design should not be easily noticeable. It should give a visitor an impression of ordinary comfort – he should not be consciously aware that some conspicuous feng shui 'tricks' or objects have been added. If you enters a house and your immediate impression is that the owner has employed feng shui, there must be something unusual or extraordinary in the design. Such design defeats the ultimate goal of feng shui, that is to create a comfortable and harmonious environment.

How to Enhance Marriage Prospects & Academic Achievements

Compared to other branches of metaphysics such as destiny analysis, feng shui is a very positive and practical tool. It provides us with knowledge about our environment, enabling us to use the various energies in our surroundings to enhance our prosperity and wellbeing. The most important goal of feng shui is to guide us to the best arrangement for our living place by exploiting the prosperous energy to create a healthy and harmonious environment. As different feng shui energies have different natures, an understanding of these energies or flying stars allows us to alter our feng shui design to suit our needs.

For example, I have explained that activating the prosperous water stars 7 or 8 increases the chance for money prosperity while sleeping in a room with the strong mountain star 7 or 8 brings stability and harmony to relationships. In this chapter, we will look at how we can use feng shui to satisfy more specific needs, such as enhancing our marriage prospects or achieving better results in school.

How to Improve Marriage Prospects

Let us look at the marriage aspect first. For many over-30 and single working ladies, a frequently asked question is, "How can I improve my chances of romance and marriage?" To help such a client, we must conduct a full inspection of her apartment and uncover the root of the problem.

In the section on the Four Pillars of Destiny, we have seen how the elements in our birth data can affect our chances of marriage. The feng shui of our house also plays a vital role. We have seen that to enhance human harmony in a house, we should sleep in a room of prosperous mountain stars. At present, these stars are symbolised by the numbers 7, 8 and 9 on the left of each square of the flying star chart. If any of these good stars are placed in an active position, such as the entrance, the livingroom or the kitchen, the human aspects in the house will be adversely affected. Our prospects for a good marriage are a vital part of the human aspects, so they are governed by the mountain stars in the flying star chart. We must thus check if such a drawback exists. If the lady has been having difficulty meeting suitable boyfriends or is having trouble developing a permanent and stable relationship, it is likely that the important mountain star 8 falls in water somewhere in the house. The mountain star 8 is a prosperous male star and the misplacement of this star in water can eliminate the possibility of developing a permanent relationship with a male partner. The first step therefore is to ensure that the mountain star 8 is well placed.

Another question to ask: Could the lady be sleeping in a room of the mountain star 7 or 9? Such rooms are good for sleeping but as these stars are female stars, they will only enhance her health and career. They will not improve her chances for meeting potential partners. The best remedy is for her to sleep in a room with the mountain star 8. If her apartment is in a newer building belonging to the Age of Seven, the room that offers the best marriage opportunity is in the N, as shown in the following flying star chart:

Flying star chart of an Age of Seven building

This building has its front facing S and its back against the N. In the N square, there are three numbers – the mountain star 8, the water star 6 and the centre number 3. From the table showing the meaning of the numbers, we can see that these are all male numbers. The number 8 refers to the youngest son, 6 the father and 3 the eldest son. Moreover, in the original Lo Shu diagram, the number 1, which refers to the middle son, is always in the N. This N square is thus full of male stars and the room is a prosperous one supported by the mountain star 8. A lady who sleeps in this room would improve her marriage chances considerably.

The number 4 carries the meaning of romance. However, as 4 is not a prosperous number today, sleeping in a room with the mountain star 4 would not enhance health or harmony in a relationship. The star may instead generate romance in a negative sense and cause emotional problems.

Besides using the good mountain star 8, we can also activate the good water star 8 which, if well placed, supports opportunities to meet more male partners. The water star 8 must be placed in an active location such as an entrance or a livingroom. If it is already well placed, we can activate its power in several ways. We can place an active object, such as a rotating clock, in the location to stir up the energy. As the number 8 is an earth element, we can also place red-coloured objects, symbolising fire, to strengthen the earth. More earth objects, such as pottery or porcelain, would help support the earth, too. To generate a stronger chance of good romance, we can place flowers in the location of the water star 8. Flowers are of the wood element and the wood can attack the earth and stir up its fighting spirit.

The Right Place to Study

Mothers are often very concerned about the 'academic position' in their home. This is the location where a student should do his studying to reap the benefits of good feng shui and enhance academic achievements. Traditionally the number 4, a wood element, is considered an academic star, and if supported by the number 1, a water element, implies good academic achievements. Many parents thus like their children to sleep or study where the flying star chart shows both 1 and 4 to be present. Unfortunately both 1 and 4 are not prosperous numbers today. When a number is not prosperous, its negative meaning supersedes its positive meaning. So staying in a room with the mountain star 1 and the water star 4, such as location E of the flying star chart in our example, may result in laziness, poor concentration in studies or even distraction by romance.

As discussed earlier, the best way to enhance human harmony is to place your child in a room with the prosperous mountain stars 7, 8 or 9. If he sleeps in one of these rooms, he will enjoy good health and harmonious relationships. But if you specifically want to enhance academic achievements, you can choose a good room with the prosperous mountain stars 7, 8 or 9 but also with implication of 1 and 4. For example, the N room in our flying star chart is almost ideal. It has the mountain star 8 to enhance health and stability and it is located in the N where the hidden Lo Shu number is 1. Only the 4 is missing.

How do we obtain the 4? Flying star feng shui is dynamic and changes over time. The flying star chart of a house shows a static picture of the built-in feng shui influence of that house. But there is more to this. In our lives, ups and downs are brought about by the changing influence of time. Besides the static flying star chart of our house, our lives are also affected by the year, month and day flying stars which are everchanging. These flying stars affect the original resident stars in the house flying star chart. For example, the year flying star chart for 1997 is shown below:

Year flying star chart for 1997

Year flying star chart for 1992

This chart shows that new stars appear in and affect all locations in our house during the year. In 1997, the year star 8 arrives in the N so our N room is under its influence. As the original mountain star of the room is also 8, the newcomer 8 reinforces the existing 8 and brings good luck to the room in 1997. A lady sleeping in such a room would certainly encounter good opportunities to get married in 1997.

The introduction of the year, month and day flying star charts thus allows us to examine events more closely. By applying the year, month and day stars, we can narrow down our feng shui analysis to check our monthly or even daily fortune. More on this in the next chapter.

Returning to our search for an appropriate place to study, if the student stays in the N room with the good support of the mountain star 8 and the hidden star 1, we can expect him to score outstanding results in the year when a 4 arrives in the N. 1992 was such a year. The 4 is an academic star that belongs to the wood element. The wood attacks the earth of 8 and stimulates its beneficial power. This is an example of how we can use the 1 and 4 combination to enhance academic achievements even when 1 and 4 are not prosperous.

In fact, good academic results can be attained even without the presence of 1 or 4 if the student sleeps in a good room. In our example, the room in the S is a good one with the double star 7. This means the room is ideal for work, study and sleep. I have observed many examples of students living in such rooms achieving top honours in public examinations.

Besides the flying stars, a good physical environment also enhances the chance of obtaining good academic results. Traditionally, a tower or tower-like object in the landscape is considered an 'academic star'. A student who is fortunate enough to stay in a room with a prosperous mountain star overlooking a tall tower outside can thus look forward to sterling academic achievements.

Forecasting Misfortunes

The most exciting aspect of flying star feng shui is how it allows us to forecast events through an understanding of the pattern of movement of the flying stars over time.

As briefly discussed in the last chapter, we can construct yearly, monthly and daily flying star charts to observe what stars are gathering in a particular location. We can then analyse the impact of this cluster of stars on the mountain or water star originally present in the flying star chart of the building. This way we can forecast events in accordance with the laws of the five elements governing the relationships between these stars. These year, month and day stars are described by the number that falls in the centre square of the chart. For 1997, for example, this number was 3. Knowing this centre number, we can then determine the numbers in the other eight directions in the nine-square chart according to the fixed pattern of the Lo Shu diagram.

Year flying star chart for 1997

The centre number of each year changes in descending order over a 10-year cycle. 1997 is 3, 1998, 2 and 1999, 1. The year 2000 sees a return to 9 and another cycle from 9 down to 1 begins. If we know the centre number for a particular year, we can easily find out the centre number for any other year before or after that year.

The monthly number that falls in the centre appears in the *The Thousand Year Calendar* which we use to find our Four Pillars of Destiny while the daily number that falls in the centre appears in the *Tong Shu*, the Chinese almanac for that year.

On any day in any location, we are therefore receiving the impact of at least four stars – the original mountain or water star in the house flying star chart plus a year star, a month star and a day star. It is the interaction of this group of four stars that brings about events at any moment in time.

A Tragic Day

Let me illustrate with an example. On 6 June 1996, at about 6 p.m., a tragedy occurred in an industrial site in the Kwai Chung area in the NW of Hong Kong. An elevator transporting workers up to construct a bridge suddenly collapsed, killing all six men inside. The number 6 featured prominently in this accident – 6/6/1996, with six men dying at about 6 p.m.

A reporter from *East* magazine interviewed me about this incident. My response: The coming together of the sixes is revealed in the flying star chart of the day. If we gather the year, month and day charts for 6/6/1996 and put them together, we obtain the following:

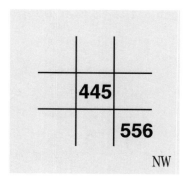

Flying star chart for 6/6/96

On 6/6/96, the calendar shows the year star 4, month star 4 and day star 5 in the centre. With these stars in the centre, the stars that gathered in the NW were 5, 5 and 6. The number 5 is the worst number, symbolising misfortune. A double 5 in the NW square indicates that an accident or misfortune will occur in this sector. In the Lo Shu diagram, the original number in the NW is 6; this trigram symbolises the father, a male. On that tragic day, the day star 6 also appeared in the NW. This symbolised that the misfortune would involve six males, perhaps all fathers …

I also made a bold prediction in the interview. Using the same technique, I predicted that a similar tragedy would occur in September, also in the NW of Hong Kong. I was right.

On 24 September 1996, in Tsuen Wan Centre in the NW of Hong Kong, another tragedy occurred when a father, in serious financial trouble, killed his entire family before committing suicide. He had sealed all the entrances and windows to his apartment and turned on the gas supply. Six bodies were found in the house. My prediction had proved correct in the location, the timing and the number of casualties. The interview, including details of the prediction, can be found in *East* magazine, issue number 190, dated 13 June 1996.

39	85	17
28	41	63
74	96	52

NW

Flying star chart for September 1996

This knowledge about the movement of the flying stars over time can help us understand our health and our fortune during any particular period. We can then take precautions by moving furniture and using decorative objects to reduce any bad influences of the flying stars.

A Health Landmine

Let us look at the following example. This is an incident that took place in the house whose feng shui we discussed in an earlier chapter, 'Checking the Feng Shui of Your Home'. Despite the generally good feng shui of this house, there are still some drawbacks – after all, no house is perfect.

The problem area is in the S which includes the master bedroom. The water star 5 which resides here is activated if we place it in a water position or active area. In our model house, the water star 5 is placed inside the bedroom, a mountain position, so it is weak and does not generate bad effects. However the air-con of the master bedroom is located in the S wall. When the air-con is turned on in the summer, it activates the water star 5 and causes ill effects. To compound matters, the father of the house liked to work in the bedroom and had placed his desk in the location of the water star 5. Thus whenever he sat there, the bad water star 5 was activated. It was like a landmine just waiting for someone to set it off.

This mine finally 'exploded' in the summer of 1993. One day the father woke up and found one ear totally deaf. His doctor delivered shocking news – his eardrum was severely damaged and there was no hope of regaining normal hearing. When he finally pulled himself together, he decided to consult a specialist. The specialist examined his ear with more sophisticated instruments and concluded that the problem was only a large piece of dirt covering his ear drum.

Let us look at the year and month charts to see why this happened:

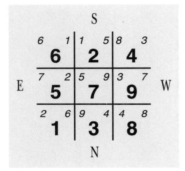

| Feng shui chart of house | Flying star chart for October 1993 |

The relevant square is in the S where he sits and works. The original mountain star 1 belongs to the water element while the original water star 5 belongs to the earth element.

In the month of the incident, a concentration of 5s and 2s – all earth elements – in the S destroyed the water of the mountain star 1. Earlier, we saw how each element is related to the parts of our body. Water is our kidneys and our ears. As water is being destroyed by the heavy concentration of earth, either the kidneys or the ears will be affected. This matches events, with the earth elements symbolising the large lump of dirt blocking his ear. Thanks to the overall good feng shui of the house, only his hearing – and not the potentially more serious kidney aspect – was affected.

Fire Tragedy

The fire tragedy that struck a branch of the Hong Kong and Shanghai Bank in Hong Kong in 1994 also demonstrates the mechanism of the flying stars. On the morning of 10 January, when the bank was packed with customers, an man

166

clutching a bottle of kerosene approached one of the bank tellers. The man was enraged because his wife had quarrelled with him and had left him the day before. Seeking the whereabouts of his wife, he threatened the bank teller, a friend of his wife, by waving the bottle of kerosene in one hand and a lighted match in the other. In the confusion, he dropped the bottle of kerosene on the ground and a fire broke out. This triggered the automatic alarm system and the front entrance was immediately sealed, trapping the staff inside. The workers attempted to escape through the back, but the back exit, through disuse, had been bricked up from the outside. The workers were soon suffocated by the heavy smoke; 13 people died.

Let us examine the feng shui chart of the bank to see how this tragedy is reflected by the flying stars.

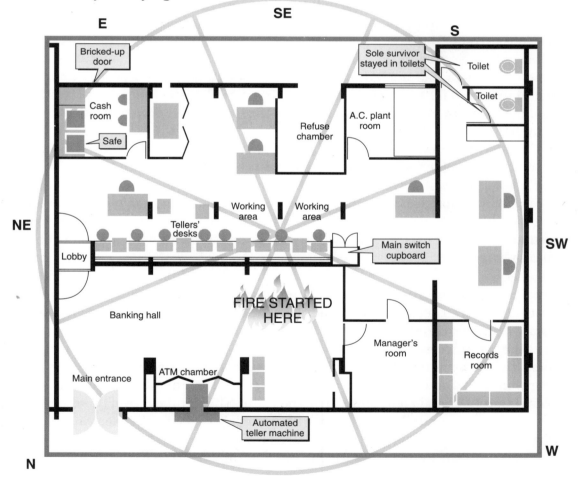

Floor plan of the bank

Flying star chart of the bank

Flying star chart for 10/1/94

Built in the Age of Five, the building faces NW. The flying star chart shows the prosperous water star 7 in the NW so this is a prosperous building facing a very busy street. The bank's main entrance, however, is not in the NW; instead it is located to one side in the N, where the water star 2 and the mountain star 9 reside. This is a bad entrance as the water star 2 is not prosperous and the mountain star 9 falls in water, and is the first sign that the human aspect is not good in this office. Moreover 9 is a symbol of fire. If not well placed, it can become a fire hazard.

Inside the bank, the lobby – the passageway leading to the office – is located in the NE. The chart shows the presence of the water star 9 and the mountain star 7 here. The water star 9 is not unfavourable but the mountain star 7 in the passageway is not good for human aspects. The remaining good mountain star, 8, is found in the S, where the toilet is located. So this good mountain star is also wasted in an unimportant location. The flying star chart thus indicates impending human tragedy.

Let us now examine the flying star chart for 10 January 1994. In the N sector, at the main entrance and the banking hall, the numbers 3, 2 and 2 appear. Three is the trigram symbolising a robber or an angry man. Two is also a bad number that carries the meaning of fire.

At this juncture, it is necessary to introduce some additional knowledge about the flying stars. We have all along considered 2 as an earth element, as determined by the Lo Shu diagram. There is, however, another important and mysterious diagram in feng shui called the Ho To. The significance of this diagram is that it presents numbers in pairs, with each pair carrying the meaning of one element. The pair of numbers 7 and 2 are found in the S sector, coinciding with the position of the number 9 in the Lo Shu diagram. As 9 is a fire element, 7 and 2 also carry the meaning of fire.

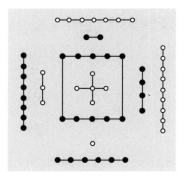

The Ho To diagram

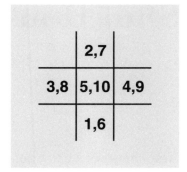

The Ho To numbers

Armed with this Ho To interpretation of the numbers, let us examine the flying star chart again. We can see two 9s in the NE, two 2s in the N and two 7s in the NW, all meaning fire, while 3 in the N is the wood element that stimulates the fire of the number 9. The flying star chart thus actually portrayed the tragic events in the bank on that day.

The worst number 5 is mostly found in the E and SE – near the bricked-up back door where most of the dead bodies were found.

Only one person survived the tragedy. She was found inside the toilet in the S sector and recovered after several weeks in hospital. The flying star chart shows that she fortunately chose the best location to hide herself because the toilet in the S sector is where the mountain star 8 was able to save her life.

Feng Shui Housekeeping

I n the last few chapters I have demonstrated that the changing flying stars over time are the actual cause of events in our house. As the flying stars are moving in a fixed pattern, their locations are clearly predictable. Knowledge about the future location and influence of these flying stars enables us not only to forecast the fortune in our house in any future month or year, but also allows us to take timely precautions to minimise bad influences, or to maximise good influences.

To make best use of the flying stars, we must thoroughly understand their nature and how they interact with one another. Like everything in the Universe, the flying stars carry with them the elements. So they are also governed by the Cycle of Birth and Cycle of Destruction of the five elements as introduced in the opening chapter of this book. The following table shows the essential elemental nature of the flying stars 1 to 9 and their equivalent colours:

Flying star No.	Element	Colour
1	Water	Black
2	Earth	Yellow
3	Wood	Green, blue
4	Wood	Green, blue
5	Earth	Yellow
6	Metal	White, gold, silver
7	Metal	White, gold, silver
8	Earth	Yellow
9	Fire	Red, purple

Elemental nature of the flying stars and their equivalent colours

How to Minimise Bad Effects and Maximise Benefits

To minimise the ill effect of a bad flying star, we must reduce the strength of the element. Conversely, if we wish to maximise the benefit of a good flying star, we must enhance the strength of that element. There are three ways to increase a star's strength:

1. We can give it a 'friend' by supporting it with the same element. For example, if we want to strengthen the water star 8, which is of the earth element, we can place more earth objects in that location. Earth supports earth so the water star 8 will become stronger.

2. We can provide a flying star with its resource element, the element that gives birth to it. For example, if we want to strengthen the water star 8, we can place red or purple objects in the location. As red and purple belong to the fire element, the resource element of the earth element 8, the 8 will become stronger.

3. A flying star also becomes stronger when under attack. For example, if we place some wood objects in the location of the water star 8, the wood, being the destructive element of earth, will attack and stir up the earth energy, thus enhancing the star's strength.

If we need to reduce the bad influence of a flying star, we can do the reverse. For example, if we find that our entrance is in the direction of the unfavourable water star 6, there are two ways we can minimise its ill effect:

1. Six is a metal number so we can exhaust its power with water. As metal gives birth to water, the energy of the metal 6 will be reduced by the water we place there.

2. We can also place wooden objects. As metal conquers wood, the metal energy of the 6 will also be exhausted by wood.

Using these simple rules, we can carry out yearly and monthly feng shui maintenance to generate the strongest prosperity and to minimise misfortune in our house. The most problematic flying stars are the bad numbers 5, 2 and 3. For example, let us look at the year flying star chart for 1997. The number 5 is located in the W, 2 in the SE and 3 in the centre. Now look at the floor plan of your home and see what rooms fall in these positions. If important areas like the main entrance, the master bedroom or the children's room are affected, we should take immediate precautions. There are traditional feng shui decorative objects available which have been designed to dissolve the ill effects of bad flying stars.

If we find the bad star 5 in an important room or at the entrance, we should be especially concerned as 5 is the worst influence that brings misfortunes. The troubles of Xinjiang province in the extreme west of China – serious earthquakes and social unrest – in 1997 are a case in point. For our home, the common remedy to the 5 is to hang a metal windchime in the affected area. This is because the 5 is an earth element and is exhausted by metal, represented by the metallic chimes of a metal windchime.

The flying star 2 symbolises sickness. If the year flying star 2 arrives at our room or entrance, the traditional way to reduce its bad effect is to hang a string of six metal coins. As 2 is an earth element, it will be exhausted by the metal represented by the metal coins. Six coins are used in the string not only because 6 is a metal number, but also because 6 originates from the trigram symbolising the father and 2 from the trigram representing the mother. If a 'mother' stirs up trouble, it is only logical to pacify her by sending the 'father'.

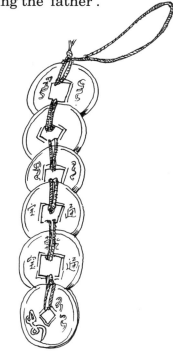

Windchime for bad star 5   Six coins for bad star 2

The flying star 3 carries the meaning of agitation, anger and robbery. If it arrives at your entrance, place a red carpet or a red-coloured picture at the door. Red is a fire element which will exhaust the wood element of the 3.

To ensure long-term health and harmony in the house, we should pay attention to the monthly changes in the flying stars as well. At the beginning of each year, check the year flying star chart and place objects such as windchimes, strings of coins or red posters in the locations of the stars 5, 2 and 3 respectively. These objects should be left there for the entire year. Then at the beginning of every month, check the calendar to see where the monthly bad stars of 5, 2 and 3 fall. Again use windchimes, metal coins and red-coloured objects to remedy the month stars. During certain months, the bad stars may double or even triple up.

For example, in 1997, the year star 5 is in the W. For the month between 5 April to 5 May 1997, the month star 5 is also in the W. This doubles the strength of the bad star 5, making the W particularly dangerous during this period. If the W is an important location in your house, such as the master bedroom or the main entrance, you should hang a metal windchime there and exercise utmost care. Another critical month in 1997 for the W location falls in the month between 8 December 1997 and 6 January 1998. This is when the month star 2 arrives in the W to join forces with the year star 5. The combination of 2 and 5 usually signals trouble or misfortune.

You will find it very worthwhile to keep a few sets of these essential feng shui objects in your home. At the beginning of each month, check the month flying star chart and ensure that you counter any bad star with the appropriate feng shui object.

A Look at 1998 and 1999

To conclude this book, let us first look at the year chart for 1998 and see what we should do to ensure a prosperous and healthy year of the Tiger, and then briefly examine the year chart for 1999. Let us assume we are living in the apartment discussed in the chapter 'Checking the Feng Shui of Your Home'.

The flying star chart for 1998 is shown below:

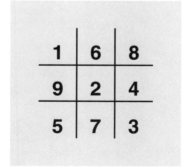

Flying star chart of house   Flying star chart for 1998

In 1998, the 2 moves to the centre and the bad star 5 shifts to the NE. The 3 falls in the NW. The floor plan shows the main door to be in the NE. We should thus hang a metal windchime to ward off the bad influence of the year star 5. This, however, is not enough as the bad water star 6 also falls in the NE entrance. A metal windchime here reduces the damage caused by the 5 but may enhance the bad influence of the 6 causing legal trouble. We should therefore also place a small bottle of water in the NE to reduce the effects of both the 5 and the 6.

The bad star 2 moves to the centre in 1998. The centre of the house is the entrance to the passageway so we should hang a string of six metal coins there to counter this bad number. The year star 3 shifts to the NW which is the livingroom, meeting the water star 8 in the house flying star chart. The 3 is a wood element which attacks the earth element of the 8, stirring up the good energy. So this looks like a prosperous year for the NW livingroom and no remedy is needed. To play it safe, however, we can still place a red carpet in the livingroom. Red, a fire element, has two good effects. The fire will exhaust the wood element of 3 and also strengthen the good earth element 8.

The good year star 8 falls in the SW, reinforcing the mountain star 8 in the master bedroom. The household can thus expect to enjoy a healthy year. But the entrance to the master bedroom is in the NE where the year star 5 also resides in 1998. A windchime and a small bottle of water should thus be placed there. With these precautions, any ill effects brought about by the changing year and month stars can be minimised.

In 1999 the flying star 1 will move to the centre. The bad star 5 will be in the S, the 2 in the NW and the 3 in the W. The focus of trouble will thus be in the S where the resident water star 5 will be reinforced by the year star 5. We must therefore minimise activities in the S in 1999 and hang a metal windchime there to lessen the chance of misfortune.

9	5	7
8	1	3
4	6	2

Flying star chart for 1999

Appendix 1

How to Convert Birth Data into the Four Pillars of Destiny

In most methods of destiny analysis, a person's fortune is identified by his birth data, which is regarded as some sort of cosmic code, able to reveal the components of our destiny. The Four Pillars of Destiny method also constructs our destiny on the basis of individual birth data, which includes the birth year, month, day and hour. This data is translated into the five basic elements – metal, wood, water, fire and earth – through the Chinese calendar. Therefore, the first step to practising the Four Pillars of Destiny is to translate a set of birth data from the Western calendar into the Chinese calendar.

The tool to perform this exercise is a book called *The Thousand Year Calendar*. It contains the conversion tables between the Western calendar and the Chinese calendar, usually covering about 130 years between 1900 to 2030. This book enables us to convert any date in the Western calendar into the form of heavenly stems and earthly branches.

The first step to using the calendar is to find the page covering the relevant year. For example, let us translate the following data into the Four Pillars:

Year   – 1993
Month – December
Day   – 13th
Hour   – 10 a.m.

Turn to the page showing the calendar for the year 1993. In the first column, you will be able to see the large Chinese characters ' 癸酉 '. These two characters represent the pillar for the year 1993.

Each column shows dates in Arabic numbers. Find the Arabic number 12/13 and you will also see the two Chinese characters ' 戊辰 ' in the same box containing '12/13'.

These two Chinese characters represent the day pillar. We have now obtained the year and day pillars.

The next step is to find out which month the date 12/13 falls into so that we can establish the month pillar as well. This is somewhat more complicated as each vertical column of *The Thousand Year Calendar* shows a month in the Chinese lunar calendar, which is different from the Hsia calendar adopted for the Four Pillars of Destiny. Therefore the commencing date on each vertical column (the box on top) is only the commencing date of the month in the lunar calendar, which is not applicable here. We need to find the commencing date in the Hsia calendar instead.

The commencing date for each month of the Hsia calendar is marked in black boxes. As our date is 12/13, we need to look back to see which is the black box prior to the date 12/13. In this example, the date 12/7 is marked in black. So 12/7 is the commencing date for the month. And 1/5 is the starting date of the following month. Hence the date 12/13 falls into a month which starts on 12/7 and ends on 1/5.

Looking up the top of the column, we can find the Chinese character '甲子' which represents the month pillar for the date 12/13.

One complication is that there are two black boxes for each month. One shows the beginning of the month while the other shows the midpoint of the month. We therefore have to be careful not to take the midpoint of the month by mistake. The key to distinguishing between the starting date and the mid date is that the starting date often falls in the range between the 1st and the 10th of the Western calendar. So a blackened date after the 10th is likely to be the mid month date, not the starting date.

Now we have the year pillar, the month pillar and the day pillar. The remaining task is to find the hour pillar. The Chinese divide the time of each day into 12 hours, represented by the 12 earthly branches. The following table shows the conversion between the Chinese hour and the Western hour. One can easily look up this table to convert Western time into Chinese hours. In our example, 10 a.m. in the table is represented by the Chinese character ' 巳 '. So this is the earthly branch of the hour pillar.

Western Time	Chinese Hour	Animal Signs
2300 – 0100	子	Rat
0100 – 0300	丑	Ox
0300 – 0500	寅	Tiger
0500 – 0700	卯	Rabbit
0700 – 0900	辰	Dragon
0900 – 1100	巳	Snake
1100 – 1300	午	Horse
1300 – 1500	未	Goat
1500 – 1700	申	Monkey
1700 – 1900	酉	Rooster
1900 – 2100	戌	Dog
2100 – 2300	亥	Pig

We have now established the year, month, day and hour pillars for the moment of time 10 a.m., 13 December 1993 as follows:

HOUR	DAY	MONTH	YEAR
?	戊 Earth	甲 Wood	癸 Water
巳 Fire	辰 Earth	子 Water	酉 Metal

However, these steps only provide seven Chinese characters. The heavenly stem of the hour pillar is still missing. The heavenly stem of the hour pillar is determined by the heavenly stem of the day pillar:

Day Pillars		Heavenly Stem of 1st Hour
甲 Yang Wood	己 Yin Earth	甲 Yang Wood
乙 Yin Wood	庚 Yang Metal	丙 Yang Fire
丙 Yang Fire	辛 Yin Metal	戊 Yang Earth
丁 Yin Fire	壬 Yang Water	庚 Yang Metal
戊 Yang Earth	癸 Yin Water	壬 Yang Water

After determining the heavenly stem of the first hour from the above table, you can locate the heavenly stems of the remaining 11 hours by counting forward. For example, if the day heavenly stem is yang metal 庚 :

1st hour —	丙 Fire	子 Water	(2300 – 0100)
2nd hour —	丁 Fire	丑 Earth	(0100 – 0300)
3rd hour —	戊 Earth	寅 Wood	(0300 – 0500)
4th hour —	己 Earth	卯 Wood	(0500 – 0700)
5th hour —	庚 Metal	辰 Earth	(0700 – 0900)
6th hour —	辛 Metal	巳 Fire	(0900 – 1100)
7th hour —	壬 Water	午 Fire	(1100 – 1300)
8th hour —	癸 Water	未 Earth	(1300 – 1500)
9th hour —	甲 Wood	申 Metal	(1500 – 1700)
10th hour —	乙 Wood	酉 Metal	(1700 – 1900)
11th hour —	丙 Fire	戌 Earth	(1900 – 2100)
12th hour —	丁 Fire	亥 Water	(2100 – 2300)

Appendix 2
How to List Out the Luck Pillars

Luck pillars are double Chinese characters derived from the month pillar. They represent the elemental influences which a person will pass through in his passage through life. Each luck pillar represents 10 years of influence. The small numbers marked on top of each luck pillar indicate the age at which a person will start coming under the influence of the luck pillar.

Let us assume the example given in the previous appendix — 10 a.m., 13 December 1993 — is the birth data of a baby girl. We can derive her first luck pillar by just taking the month pillar (甲子) and moving both the heavenly stems and earthly branches forward by a space. According to the table of the 10 heavenly stems and 12 earthly branches, the first luck pillar then becomes 乙丑. We can again move one space forward to the second luck pillar which is 丙寅, and repeat the procedure to find the third luck pillar and so on. We normally list out seven luck pillars as the life span of a person is around 70 years.

When listing out the luck pillars, it is important to distinguish between male and female, as the direction of movement of the luck pillars is different for men and women. The following rules apply:

Male born in yang year	– move forward
Male born in yin year	– move backward
Female born in yang year	– move backward
Female born in yin year	– move forward

Yang years mean singular or odd years; yin years mean plural or even years. For instance, 甲, the first heavenly stem, is yang and 乙, the second heavenly stem, is yin. By the same token, 子, the first earthly branch, is yang, and 丑, the second earthly branch, is yin.

In our example, as 1993, 癸酉, is a yin year, and this is a baby girl, the luck pillars move forward. If it is a boy, a male born in a yin year, the luck pillars should move backward instead. Then the first luck pillar for the boy will be 癸亥, one space backward from the heavenly stem and earthly branch of the month pillar 甲子. The second luck pillar will be 壬戌, another space backward.

The last step is to enter the age at which each luck pillar takes effect. Three days in a month is considered a year of age. In our case, since the baby girl was born on 13 December 1993, the rule for setting up her luck pillar is to move forward. We should count the number of days forward until we reach the end of the month, which is 5 January 1994, as indicated by the black box in *The Thousand Year Calendar*. Between her birthday 13 December and 5 January, there are about 23 days. Twenty three divided by 3 is roughly 8. This means that the baby girl will come under the influence of the first luck pillar 乙丑 from the age of 8. As each luck pillar will govern for about 10 years, she will be affected by the second luck pillar from the age of 18, the third luck pillar from the age of 28 and so on.

In the case of a baby boy born in 1993, the luck pillars will move backward. We count the number of days backward from the date of birth until we reach the starting date of the month. In our example, the previous black box showing the starting date of the month falls on 7 December.

There are roughly six days between 7 December and 13 December. As three days represent one year, dividing six by three gives us two years. So the boy will come under the influence of his first luck pillar 癸亥 at the age of two. The second luck pillar 壬戌 will start at the age of 12, the third luck pillar will commence at the age of 22 and so on. The following is the full set of Four Pillars of Destiny and luck pillars for a boy born at 10 a.m., 13 December 1993:

HOUR	DAY	MONTH	YEAR
丁 Fire	戊 Earth	甲 Wood	癸 Water
巳 Fire	辰 Earth	子 Water	酉 Metal

62	52	42	32	22	12	2
丁 Fire	戊 Earth	己 Earth	庚 Metal	辛 Metal	壬 Water	癸 Water
巳 Fire	午 Fire	未 Earth	申 Metal	酉 Metal	戌 Earth	亥 Water

If it is a baby girl, the luck pillars will move forward, starting at the age of 8, as described earlier.

Appendix 3

How to Find Relationships in a Set of Four Pillars

1. To Find Relatives

Human relationships are symbolised in two ways in a set of Four Pillars of Destiny. They can be found by means of:

* Houses – the location in a set of Four Pillars of Destiny
* Stars – by the elemental relationship with the self as represented by the heavenly stem of the day pillar.

A. Houses:

HOUR	DAY	MONTH	YEAR
Son	Self	Father	Grandfather
Daughter	Spouse	Mother	Grandmother

For example, the heavenly stem of the month pillar always symbolises the father while the earthly branch of the month pillar symbolises the mother.

B. Stars:

As the heavenly stem of the day pillar represents the self, other relatives can be represented by other elements according to their relations with the self. The following are the rules for finding relatives, if the self is a male:

Mother	– the element that gives birth to the self
Father	– the element that is destroyed by the self
Offsprings	– the element that destroys the self
Wife	– the element that is destroyed by the self (same as the father)
Brothers/sisters	– the element same as the self

What if the self is not male but female? The father, mother and brother/ sisters can still be found the same way. However, the husband and the offsprings must be found differently.

Husband   – the element that destroys the self

Offsprings   – the element that the self gives birth to

The following, where the self is a wood man/wood woman, is an example:

	Self (wood man)	Self (wood woman)
Father	Earth	Earth
Mother	Water	Water
Wife	Earth	—
Husband	—	Metal
Offspring	Metal	Fire
Brother/sister	Wood	Wood

We can find other relationships according to the cycles of birth and destruction of the five elements. For example, if we want to find the father-in-law of the above wood man, the logic is that the father-in-law is the father of his wife. As his wife is earth, the father of an earth woman is the element that she destroys. So it is water that symbolises the father-in-law of the wood man.

When assessing the fortune of a relative from a set of Four Pillars of Destiny, we need to examine both the houses and the stars symbolising that relative. For example, to check the health of our father from our own set of Four Pillars of Destiny, examine the heavenly stem of the month pillar, as well as the element that is destroyed by the self. In our example of a wood man, this element is earth. If both are unfavourable the father could suffer from ill health.

2. To Find Different Aspects Of Life

The following cover the major aspects of life: Money, Power and Status, Authority and Resources, Aspiration and Intelligence, Colleagues and Friends. They can be found according to the elemental relationships with the self.

The rules to find these aspects are:

Money   – the element that the self destroys

Power and status   – the element that destroys the self

Authority and resources – the element that gives birth to the self

Aspiration and intelligence – the element that the self gives birth to

Colleagues, friends   – the element same as the self

For example, if the self is metal, the following represent his aspects of life:

Money	– Wood
Authority and resources	– Earth
Aspiration and intelligence	– Water
Power and status	– Fire
Colleagues, friends	– Metal

The following tables show the relationships and various aspects of life for persons of each of the five elements.

1. A METAL MAN

Element	Persons	Areas of Life
Metal	Self	Colleagues, competition
Earth	Mother	Resources, support, authority
Wood	Wife, father	Wealth, money
Fire	Son	Status, pressure, power
Water	—	Intelligence, expression

2. A WOOD MAN

Element	Persons	Areas of Life
Wood	Self	Colleagues, competition
Water	Mother	Resources, support, authority
Earth	Wife, father	Wealth, money
Metal	Son	Status, pressure, power
Fire	—	Intelligence, expression

3. A WATER MAN

Element	Persons	Areas of Life
Water	Self	Colleagues, competition
Metal	Mother	Resources, support, authority
Fire	Wife, father	Wealth, money
Earth	Son	Status, pressure, power
Wood	—	Intelligence, expression

4. A FIRE MAN

Element	Persons	Areas of Life
Fire	Self	Colleagues, competition
Wood	Mother	Resources, support, authority
Metal	Wife, father	Wealth, money
Water	Son	Status, pressure, power
Earth	—	Intelligence, expression

5. AN EARTH MAN

Element	Persons	Areas of Life
Earth	Self	Colleagues, competition
Fire	Mother	Resources, support, authority
Water	Wife, father	Wealth, money
Wood	Son	Status, pressure, power
Metal	—	Intelligence, expression

Note that a metal man is defined as a man with the heavenly stem of his day pillar belonging to the metal element. The same definition applies to the other four elements. The tables above show the relationships for a male. For a female, the only differences are the relationships with the husband and the son. The following supplementary table lists the husband and son for all five types of females:

Self	Son	Husband
Metal woman	Water	Fire
Wood woman	Fire	Metal
Water woman	Wood	Earth
Fire woman	Earth	Water
Earth woman	Metal	Wood

The reasoning is that since a woman literally gives birth to her son, the element that is given birth by the self is the son. Ancient society also considered women the submissive sex to be conquered by the male. So the element that conquers the self is the husband. In all other aspects, the elemental relationships follow the patterns shown earlier.

How to Draw the Flying Star Charts

1 Determine the Age of the house and write the age number in the centre of a nine square chart. Then place the other eight numbers according to the Lo Shu pattern. The example below is an Age of Six building:

5	1	3
4	6	8
9	2	7

2 Determine the front and back direction of the house and enter the two numbers representing the two directions into the centre square. The back number is on the left while the front number on the right. For example, for an Age of Six building with its back against the east and the front facing west, the number 4 represents the east and the number 8 represents the west:

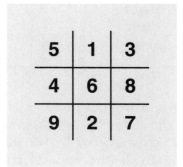

186

3 Determine the pattern of movement of the two middle numbers, either forward or backward, according to the following dial:

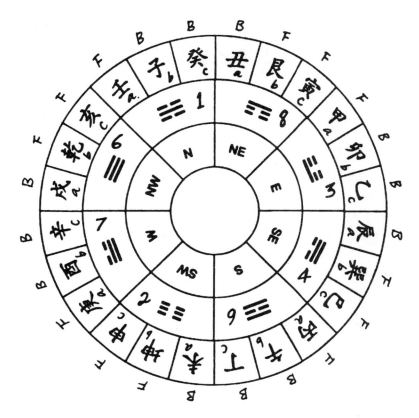

For example, if the measured direction of the above building is right east (back), right west (front), the characters in the Lo Pan are 卯 (Back) 酉 (Front). The two numbers entered in the centre of the nine square chart are 4 and 8.

From the dial, if you look up the number 4, you will find three 4s – 4a, 4b and 4c – as there are three mountains to each direction. We select the middle one in this case, as the middle one means 'right'. However, if the measured direction is not 'right east' but leaning towards NE, we have to select 4a. After selecting 4b, the F indicates it is a forward movement pattern. So you should place the other numbers in ascending order in the other squares, in the order of 4, 5, 6, 7, 8, 9, 1, 2 and 3.

Now look up the number 8 in the dial. Select 8b. The indication is F, so the movement is in ascending order of 8, 9, 1, 2, 3, 4, 5, 6 and 7. If you see B, the movement is backward and descending, so you should count 8, 7, 6, 5, 4, 3, 2, 1 and 9.

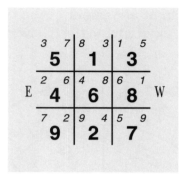

Flying star chart for an Age of Six house facing exact west

4 What if the centre small number is 5? You will not be able to find a 5 on the dial. Instead, the Age number should be used to determine the forward or backward movement of the 5. For example, for a SE-NW house of Age of Six, but leaning to E-W, the 5 in the SE goes to the centre. Then you should look up 6a in the diagram. The indication is B so the movement should be backward and descending, that is, 5, 4, 3, 2, 1, 9, 8, 7 and 6.

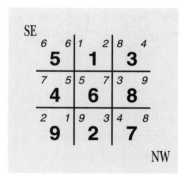

Flying star chart for an Age of Six house facing northwest

Appendix 5

Flying Star Charts for Age of Seven Buildings

The 16 charts which follow show the feng shui flying star distributions for Age of Seven buildings (buildings completed between 1984 and 2003 inclusive). The following are brief guidelines for using these charts:

1. Find out the accurate direction of the building by means of a Lo Pan.
2. Mark down the Chinese characters taken from the Lo Pan and check their English equivalents from the simplified Lo Pan on the following page.
3. Then find the chart applicable to buildings of that direction in this appendix.

Example

By standing facing the front of a house, holding the Lo Pan horizontally, the magnetic needle points to a direction indicated by the Chinese characters 丁 and 癸 . This means the back of the building is facing the direction 丁 and the front is facing the direction 癸 . From the Lo Pan on the following page, we can see that 丁 is S2 and 癸 is N2. The applicable flying star chart for such a building is therefore S2-N2, meaning a building with its back facing the S2 direction and its front facing the N2 direction.

Please refer to the 'Feng Shui' section of this book for detailed interpretations of the numbers on the charts. Note that these charts are applicable to Age of Seven buildings only.

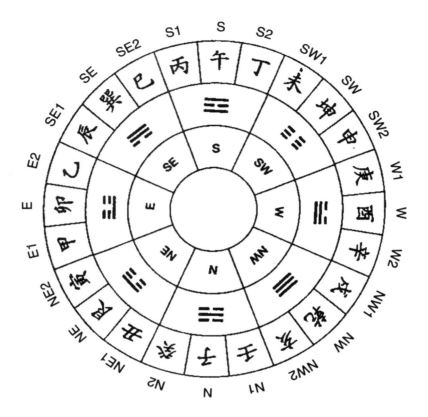

Fig. A The Lo Pan showing the 24 mountains

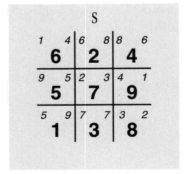

S1-N1   S-N, S2-N2

S

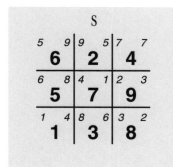

	S	
5 9	9 5	7 7
6	**2**	**4**
6 8	4 1	2 3
5	**7**	**9**
1 4	8 6	3 2
1	**3**	**8**

SW1–NE1

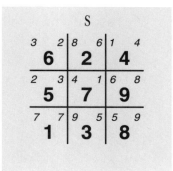

	S	
3 2	8 6	1 4
6	**2**	**4**
2 3	4 1	6 8
5	**7**	**9**
7 7	9 5	5 9
1	**3**	**8**

SW–NE, SW2–NE2

	S	
8 4	4 9	6 2
6	**2**	**4**
7 3	9 5	2 7
5	**7**	**9**
3 8	5 1	1 6
1	**3**	**8**

W1–E1

	S	
1 6	5 1	3 8
6	**2**	**4**
2 7	9 5	7 3
5	**7**	**9**
6 2	4 9	8 4
1	**3**	**8**

W–E, W2–E2

	S	
9 7	4 2	2 9
6	**2**	**4**
1 8	8 6	6 4
5	**7**	**9**
5 3	3 1	7 5
1	**3**	**8**

NW1–SE1

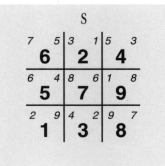

	S	
7 5	3 1	5 3
6	**2**	**4**
6 4	8 6	1 8
5	**7**	**9**
2 9	4 2	9 7
1	**3**	**8**

NW–SE, NW2–SE2

N1-S1

S

^{2 3} **6**	^{7 7} **2**	^{9 5} **4**
^{1 4} **5**	^{3 2} **7**	^{5 9} **9**
^{6 8} **1**	^{8 6} **3**	^{4 1} **8**

N-S, N2-S2

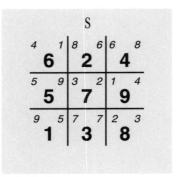

S

^{4 1} **6**	^{8 6} **2**	^{6 8} **4**
^{5 9} **5**	^{3 2} **7**	^{1 4} **9**
^{9 5} **1**	^{7 2} **3**	^{2 3} **8**

NE1-SW1

S

^{9 5} **6**	^{5 9} **2**	^{7 7} **4**
^{8 6} **5**	^{1 4} **7**	^{3 2} **9**
^{4 1} **1**	^{6 8} **3**	^{2 3} **8**

NE-SW, NE2-SW2

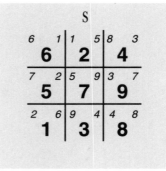

S

^{2 3} **6**	^{6 8} **2**	^{4 1} **4**
^{3 2} **5**	^{1 4} **7**	^{8 6} **9**
^{7 7} **1**	^{5 9} **3**	^{9 5} **8**

E1-W1

S

^{4 8} **6**	^{9 4} **2**	^{2 6} **4**
^{3 7} **5**	^{5 9} **7**	^{7 2} **9**
^{8 3} **1**	^{1 5} **3**	^{6 1} **8**

E-W, E2-W2

S

^{6 1} **6**	^{1 5} **2**	^{8 3} **4**
^{7 2} **5**	^{5 9} **7**	^{3 7} **9**
^{2 6} **1**	^{9 4} **3**	^{4 8} **8**

SE1-NW1

SE-NW, SE2-NW2

The Author

Raymond Lo, popularly known as 'Feng Shui Lo' in Hong Kong, is a professional feng shui researcher and practitioner. His experience also covers the Four Pillars of Destiny and the predictions of the I Ching Oracle.

After graduating with a degree in Social Sciences from the University of Hong Kong, Mr Lo's interest in feng shui led him to seriously study the ancient art. He subsequently learnt to explain the complicated theories of Chinese metaphysics in a concise and logical manner, using this skill to write a popular feng shui column in *The Hong Kong Standard* between 1988 and 1991. In this column he made several forecasts about world events, including the outbreak and the result of the Gulf War, the fall of Mikhail Gorbachev and Margaret Thatcher's resignation, all of which later proved to be accurate.

Mr Lo is the author of *Feng Shui & Destiny for Managers* and *Feng Shui: The Pillars of Destiny* and has published several other feng shui titles in Chinese. He frequently contributes his knowledge of feng shui to various media publications. He has appeared on international TV programmes such as the BBC's *Whicker's World* and ABC's *Good Morning America* and has been interviewed by media networks such as CNN, ABN, CNBC and RTHK.

He is a feng shui lecturer at the School of Professional and Continual Education in the University of Hong Kong. Mr Lo is also a consultant to the Hong Kong Tourist Association for their annual Health and Fortune Expo and Feng Shui Tour, the Peninsula Hotel's Peninsula Academy and the *South China Morning Post*'s feng shui hotline.

Feng Shui & Destiny for Managers
Raymond Lo

Business successes attributed to good feng shui are legion in the Far East. But what exactly is feng shui? Or, for that matter, destiny? How are these techniques employed in business? Can you learn to apply these methods to your own needs and thus gain an important advantage in the business world?

The answer is a resounding YES! In this book, internationally renowned feng shui expert Raymond Lo unveils the secrets behind the mysterious Chinese arts of feng shui, the Four Pillars of Destiny and the I Ching Oracle and offers invaluable step-by-step advice on how you can manage every aspect of your business or managerial career to greater heights of success.

Using famous personalities ranging from Hong Kong billionaire Li Ka-shing and Hollywood superstar Arnold Schwarzenegger to shipping magnate Sir Y. K. Pao and former U.S. President Richard Nixon, he demonstrates convincingly how you can:

- Choose the business or career most favourable to your destiny to ensure success
- Pinpoint the best time to invest in any venture
- Team up with winning business partners
- Hire and manage employees successfully
- Forecast prosperity in the stock market
- Choose and design a prosperous office
- Analyse business risks and uncertainties with confidence
- Select auspicious dates for important business occasions

Feng Shui: The Pillars of Destiny
Raymond Lo

Power, wealth, fame, success – are our fates merely left to the vagaries of change?

Now, Raymond Lo offers us a rare chance to unravel the secrets behind the mysterious arts of feng shui and the Four Pillars of Destiny, for centuries known only to a few privileged scholars of classical Chinese metaphysics and philosophy. In a clear and logical fashion this renowned expert leads us step-by-step through the principles and techniques of feng shui analysis. Using famous buildings and places as practical examples, he demonstrates how this ancient theory has a very real relevance to modern life, affecting everything from financial success to health and happiness.

In the second part of this book he reveals how the details of our individual birth data, expressed in the Four Pillars of Destiny, hold the key to predicting our future fortunes. Follow the rise and fall of world-famous personalities and understand the tragedies and successes of the rich and famous. What made Ronald Li a millionaire? Why did George Bush lose the Presidential Election? Did Elvis commit suicide? Whether your interest lies in the world of big business, power and riches, or in romance, fame and health, *Feng Shui: The Pillars of Destiny* opens the door to understanding your past, present and future.